RESTLESS BONE

Edited by

JACQUI ROWE

ELAINE CHRISTIE

© 2014 Elaine Catherine Christie
Poems © individual authors as appropriate
ISBN: 978-1-63315-204-5

Printed by Book Printing UK
Remus House, Coltsfoot Drive, Peterborough, PE2 9B

In memory
of
Pat Clarke

ACKNOWLEDGEMENTS

This journey has been a real labour of love for poetry and animals, and a desire to educate others of the horrors that lie beyond our four walls and that it is us up to each of us to do our part. This book is dedicated to help fight the fur trade in all its forms.

There are many to thank for getting me to this point, starting with Julie Boden and Matt Nunn, passing on their poetry wisdom and encouraging me to find my voice through poetry. To Helen Calcutt, David Calcutt and Richard Bonfield; their poetry continues to inspire me and has also influenced me to join Born Free Foundation. To George and Joy Adamson together with Elsa who delighted me so with their life story that I fell in love with lions. For the actors who played their part in 'Born Free' film, Virginia McKenna, Bill Travers, it remains my number one film. Thank you to them, to Will Travers and everyone at Born Free Foundation for their endurance in making the world a better place for wildlife. Thank you to Josephine Wall for letting us include some of her beautiful fantasy art, to enhance our words. To Jacqui Rowe for her contribution and for her expertise in editing this book, I trust her magic eye! Thanks to Saleha Begum, Tessa Lowe and Debbie Aldous for their influence and invaluable experience. Thank you to Janine Allen, Ann Berlin and The Animal Liberation Front. To all the poets in this book, some of which I have seen perform for many years, some whom - I have worked with and others who are recent friends, I am as passionate about your poems as you are, well done and thank you for coming together to create a stunning anthology and being a voice for the voiceless.

Thank you to Book Printing UK for producing this publication.

Elaine Catherine Christie

FOREWORD

In the long litany of suffering we as a species have inflicted on the animal kingdom over the past 5 thousand years of so-called civilisation the iniquities of the fur trade in all its variegated forms occupy an especially barbarous position.

The suffering associated with traps, which can lead to a long and lingering death, is now compounded by the factory farming of fur on an industrial scale. And this is especially the case in China where a long history of indifference to animal welfare is now allied to a desire to live the lifestyle of the affluent West.

The feeding of live goats to tigers, the skinning alive of rabbits, cats and dogs, these and many more casual cruelties, such as the ongoing suffering of the moon bears, stains and sustains a whole culture; but we in the west can hardly hold our heads up high, when similar cruelties are meted out behind a thousand closed doors and new atrocities appear in the papers on a regular basis.

As honorary poet in residence for the Born Free Foundation I am of course delighted to recommend this collection as an impassioned call for animal alms.

As far as I am concerned animals should be free to express their inner natures and make use of the marvellous and in many cases mysterious faculties with which they explore their own particular worlds.

Any infringement of these liberties precludes the living of a natural life.

In Restless Bones Elaine Christie has gathered together a formidable array of artists and poets to make her anguished case and let us hope that the next sea change in humanity's collective unconscious will be a recognition that animals are not our suffering servants and anguished slaves but complete and magical fellow travellers in their own mysterious right.

Anyone who has read Philip Hoare's *Leviathan* will understand that this is a battle that can be won. For centuries whales were hunted as a commodity and their light and oil helped to power the industrial revolution. However with advances in scientific understanding a recognition began to dawn that whales, as sentient creatures could not be left out of our circle of concern.

Animal Rights are now in the dock and it is up to us both as individual and as a collective to make sure that the jury of the human race ensures this circle of concern is widened to include the whole of the animal kingdom.

The world is poised on the brink of the abyss but we still have time to draw back and build a brighter and a kinder future.

We may face the future as E P Thompson once said, "with a pessimism of the intellect but an optimism of the will" However *where there's a will there's a way.* And for those who envisage a kinder, gentler and ultimately more sustainable world the moving words and ethereal images presented here are a very good place to start.

Born Free Poet in Residence
Richard Bonfield
www.richardbonfieldpoet@live.co.uk

ELLA WHEELER WILCOX

The Voice of the Voiceless

I am the voice of the voiceless;
    Through me the dumb shall speak;
Till the deaf world's ear be made to hear
    The cry of the wordless weak.
From street, from cage, and from kennel,
    From jungle and stall, the wail
Of my tortured kin proclaims the sin
    Of the mighty against the frail.

I am a ray from the centre;
    And I will feed God's spark,
Till a great light glows in the night and shows
    The dark deeds done in the dark.
And full on the thoughtless sleeper
    Shall flash its glaring flame,
Till he wakens to see what crimes may be
    Cloaked under an honoured name.

The same Force formed the sparrow
    That fashioned man, the king;
The God of the Whole gave a spark of soul
    To furred and to feathered thing.
And I am my brother's keeper,
    And I will fight his fight,
And speak the word for beast and bird,
    Till the world shall set things right.

Let no voice cavil at Science--
    The strong torch-bearer of God;
For brave are his deeds, though dying creeds,
    Must fall where his feet have trod.
But he who would trample kindness
    And mercy into the dust--
He has missed the trail, and his quest will fail:
    He is not the guide to trust.

For love is the true religion,
    And love is the law sublime;
And all that is wrought, where love is not,
    Will die at the touch of time.
And Science, the great revealer,
    Must flame his torch at the Source;
And keep it bright with that holy light,
    Or his feet shall fail on the course.

Oh, never a brute in the forest,
    And never a snake in the fen,
Or ravening bird, starvation stirred,
    Has hunted its prey like men.
For hunger, and fear, and passion
    Alone drive beasts to slay,
But wonderful man, the crown of the plan,
    Tortures, and kills, for play.

He goes well fed from his table;
    He kisses his child and wife;
Then he haunts a wood, till he orphans a brood,
    Or robs a deer of its life.
He aims at a speck in the azure;

    Winged love, that has flown at a call;
It reels down to die, and he lets it lie;
    His pleasure was seeing it fall.

And one there was, weary of laurels,
    Of burdens and troubles of State;
So the jungle he sought, with the beautiful thought
    Of shooting a she lion's mate.
And one came down from the pulpit,
    In the pride of a duty done,
And his cloth sufficed, as his emblem of Christ,
    While murder smoked out of his gun.

One strays from the haunts of fashion
    With an indolent, unused brain;
But his sluggish heart feels a sudden start
    In the purpose of giving pain.
And the fluttering flock of pigeons,
    As they rise on eager wings,
From prison to death, bring a catch in his breath:
    Oh, the rapture of killing things!

Now, this is the race as we find it,
    Where love, in the creed, spells hate;
And where bird and beast meet a foe in the priest
    And in rulers of fashion and State.
But up to the Kingdom of Thinkers
    Has risen the cry of our kin;
And the weapons of thought are burnished and brought
    To clash with the bludgeons of sin.

Far Christ, of a million churches,
    Come near to the earth again;
Be more than a Name; be a living Flame;
    'Make Good' in the hearts of men.
Shine full on the path of Science,
    And show it the heights above,
Where vast truths lie for the searching eye
    That shall follow the torch of love.

CONTENTS

QUOTATIONS..1
VIRGINIA MCKENNA..3
RICHARD BONFIELD..6
JANINE ALLEN..12
MIKE ALMA..14
JUDE ASHWORTH..20
DAVID BARBER...23
WILLIAM BLAKE...26
ELIZABETH BARRETT BROWNING.....................................27
LORD BYRON...29
DAVID CALCUTT...31
HELEN CALCUTT..36
G. K. CHESTERTON...39
CHYI YU...40
ELAINE CATHERINE CHRISTIE...41
EMILY DICKINSON..46
DES – LONE WOLF..49
EUGENE EGAN...50
GIOVANNI SPOZ ESPOSITO...53
CHRIS FEWINGS...56
CAROLINE GILL..59
OLIVER WENDELL HOLMES..62
RANGZEB HUSSAIN..63
SARAH JAMES...71
JANET JENKINS..77
NINA LEWIS..80
TESSA LOWE...86
CHARLOTTE MEW..89
MATT NUNN..91
ANTONY OWEN...92
MALINI PATEL...95
JADE PHIPPS...98
CLARE POWERS..100
CHRISTINA ROSSETTI..101
JACQUI ROWE..102

ALFRED LORD TENNYSON..106
CLAIRE WALKER...107
JAN WATTS...110
WILLIAM WORDSWORTH...113
TOM WYRE..114
BIOGRAPHIES...121
CONTRIBUTORS..128

We need another wiser and perhaps a more mystical concept of animals. Remote from universal nature, and living by complicated artifice, man in civilisation surveys the creature through the glass of his knowledge and sees thereby a feather magnified and the whole image in distortion. We patronise them for their incompleteness, for their tragic fate of having taken form so far below ourselves. And therein we err, and greatly err. **For the animal shall not be measured by man. In a world older and more complete than ours they move finished and complete**, gifted with extensions of the senses we have lost or never attained, living by voices we shall never hear. They are not brethren, they are not underlings; they are other nations, caught with ourselves in the net of life and time, fellow prisoners of the splendour and travail of the earth.

Henry Beston

A thing of beauty is a joy forever.
John Keats

The pursuit of truth and beauty is a sphere of activity in which
We are permitted to remain children all our lives.
Albert Einstein

Beauty is in the heart of the beholder.
H.G. Wells

Keep close to Nature's heart… and break clear away,
Once in a while, and climb a mountain or spend a week
in the woods. Wash your spirit clean. None of Nature's
Landscapes are ugly so long as they are wild.
John Muir

Clear your mind of can't.
Samuel Johnson

Of all the creatures that were made, man is the most detestable. Of the entire bridge he is the only one - the solitary one - that possesses malice. That is the basest of all instincts, passions, vices - the most hateful. He is the only creature that has pain for sport, knowing it to be pain. Also in the list he is the only creature that has a nasty mind.

Mark Twain

When a man wants to murder a tiger he calls it sport; when a Tiger wants to murder him he calls it ferocity.
George Bernard Shaw

You must be the change you want to see in the world.
Mahatma Gandhi

I am only one, but still I am one. I cannot do everything, but still I can do something; and because I cannot do everything, I will not refuse to do something that I can do.
Helen Keller

*Only if we understand can we care.
Only if we care will we help.
Only if we help shall they be saved.*
Jane Goodall

*When I despair, I remember that all through history the ways of truth and love have always won. There have been tyrants and murderers, and for a time they can seem invincible, but in the end they always fall.
Think of it – always.*
Mahatma Gandhi

The Darkest Day

I made this journey aware
Of what I would find. Would see.
I thought I was prepared.
But nothing can. No film. No words.
Nor these few lines of mine
Can wrench your heart and haunt your mind
As seeing it yourself. Feeling it yourself.

No words can really tell you.
Should I say torment?
Cruelty? Despair? Hell on earth?
Shall I say prison? Torture?
Nightmare? Madhouse?
Nothing screams out the obscenity
Of those barbaric traps...
Yes. Traps of bars- above,
Beside, beneath, no floor
On which to rest those
Rotting, yellowed feet...
The feet of bears who carry
Still the precious moons emblazoned
On their night-dark chests.

That moon is all they have.
There is no sun to lighten
That grim shed, no trees
To soothe the eye, no wind
To stir their fur, no hope
Of kinder days. And why?
It is the bile. Of course, it is the bile.
Extracted, traded, packaged
And sold in pretty phials
For "mankind's" benefit. No kindness here.

Some bears are mad. I know
The signs too well. They sway and rock
And twist. Seeking oblivion.
Even for a minute. Even for a moment.

And then, oh God, this bear I saw.
A huge great glorious beast
Stretched out across the bars.
His back legs up against the side,
His two front legs reached high,
As if to heaven, stretched high and still
Until, suddenly, a paw dropped down
And grabbed his slavering tongue,
And pulled and pulled it out
And out again until I thought
It surely would snap free.
But no, the paw jerked up
Once more - and on and on again.

These dark satanic sheds
Are known as farms. Death Row
I say. Outside the owners offer tea.
I want to put them in a cage
And let them cry. In vain.

Not all these innocent creatures
Will find sanctuary. There are thousands.

Only a few will walk on grass,
Climb trees, feel sun and wind. Be loved.

And, as I stood, aghast, the eye
Of one sweet bear looked into mine.

Unflinching. Enduring. Stoic.
Yes, that is the word I seek.
I heard it many times. The stoicism
Of these great animals. And, miraculously,
The rescued ones appear to feel
No malice, bear no grudge, as if
They sense the kindness shown
The affection given.

In all the years I have watched
Imprisoned animals - some neglected,
Some abused, some stir-crazy,
All helpless - this November day
Has been the darkest of them all.
And what a lesson have I learned.
How dare I now complain of cold,
Or tiredness, or waiting for a train?
On behalf of all who cause
This purgatory, I hang my head in shame
And beg the bears' forgiveness in my heart.

Virginia McKenna
Founder & Trustee
Born Free Foundation

RICHARD BONFIELD

Africa's Reflected Glory

The Cheetah is all glide and guile
A knife
Slicing the buttery savannah
The sun with silver claws

Running on Apollo's leash of light
Tearing up the raw and bleeding dawn
With fangs of smoking gold
With eyes of flaming umber
It hunts with its brothers in beauty
A dappled pack of amber stealth
Raiding the savannah's leaping wealth
In swirling velvet unison

But it tires easily
It has no stomach for a fight
And - once wounded by its wide eyed struggling game
It swiftly returns to the fires from whence it came

But there are - sadly less natural ways to tame the morning
"Yes today for five thousand pounds
You can purchase the sun's fur

And wrap yourself in Africa's reflected glory

Yes today for a mere five thousand pounds

You can wear the stole of Kenya

And dance without a care

Now do I hear five or ah yes six thousand pounds

From you catwalk queens out there!"

Bush Meat   6 Degrees of Separation

In the corner of the fly blown market
They hang like Nero's Christians
Francis Bacon's screaming Popes
Swinging burn out crucifixions
On a butcher's slab
A hand reaches out imploringly
Its fingers so like our own
But here the meat God has spoken
A difference in degrees is a difference in kind
And here the difference is death
Although it is a kind of cannibalism
The six degrees of separation
Render the flesh acceptable
The act permissible
And so the hands - arms - legs and torsos
Swing in this grotesque diss assembly
It is more like a morgue than a market
The autopsy room on the island of Doctor Moreau
But one cannot deny that the flesh is special
One does not get to eat one's distant cousins every day
And so the flesh is purified and sanctified by the saints
And eaten in celebration of the resurrection
It is the ambrosial food of the meat Gods

Relished in the quiet of the dark confessional.

Do Not Go Gently

The polar bear is treading on thin ice
Walking on frosty eggshells
Waiting for his frozen savannah
To crystallize
For the moment he is in purgatory
He has a passport
But no country
A borderline case
Perfected for a non-existent landscape
He scavenges on the edge of his ghostly dominion
Which is melting beyond his reach
A down and out on skid row
He lumbers amongst the trash cans
A frosty Grendel on the edge of sight
He blunders outside the oil fired mead hall of humanity
Under the pipelines of black gold
He rages – dirty woolly bear white
A species at the end of his tether
He rages under the borealis
RAGES – RAGES – RAGES
Against the dying of the ice.

An Elegy for the South China Tiger

No longer will this sheet of flame
Come padding through the Chinese rain
No longer will this work of art
Inspire us with its jungle craft
A creature now consigned to myth
Becomes a number on a list
A ghostly calligraphic script

Whose pug marks vanish into mist
We hunt in vain for sight or sound
Whose scent is lost – cannot be found
Though represented everywhere
On temple scrolls and clothes and chairs
There are no tigers left at all
Beyond the temple's boundary walls
What lived and breathed and fought and thrived
Was twelve feet four and three feet wide
Is now a picture in a book
A pictogram
A frozen look
That gazes out from yesterday
Which now seems very far away
"And was it real?" the daughter asks
"Did Noah save it on the ark?
Or was it just a magic tale
Like Jonah and the giant whale"
"I saw it," said the daughter's dad
"When I was just a little lad
It was the most amazing thing
With stars for eyes and fire for skin
But we have let it slip away
Across the fields and far away."
The girl looked sad
The father sighed
And so it was the tiger died
We hunt in vain for sight or sound
Though represented everywhere
On temple scrolls and clothes and chairs
There are no tigers left at all
Beyond the temple's boundary walls
What lived and breathed and fought and thrived
Was twelve feet four and three feet wide
Is now a picture in a book
A pictogram
A frozen look
That gazes out from yesterday

Which now seems very far away
And in the taxidermist's case
We see the tiger face to face
But see no star and feel no fire
Just bolsters stuffed with chicken wire
And glass eyes where the stars all shone
Because we shot them – every one
Without a shadow of a doubt
And let the tiger's fire go out.

The South China Tiger is now extinct, according to the Zoological Society of London. It is the fourth sub species to become extinct within a century and is, According to tiger experts the ancestor of all other sub species. Specimens Remain in zoos, but these are all cross breeds and not true to type.

Horse Whisperer

For G.K. Chesterton

I was the ass that bucked and brayed
Before the crowds that wept and prayed

Upon my back a gentle man
Reached out his gently loving hand

He calmed me with a whispered kiss
I never knew a man like this…

The palm fronds gently paved our way
Before he left he gave me hay

And said he'd come to whisper signs
To tame all men and make them kind

Then said he'd been – in Herod's time
A stable boy from Palestine.

JANINE ALLEN

I Rescued a Human Today

I rescued a human today.

Her eyes met mine as she walked down the corridor peering apprehensively into the kennels. I felt her need instantly and knew I had to help her. I wagged my tail, not too exuberantly, so she wouldn't be afraid.

As she stopped at my kennel I blocked her view from a little accident I had in the back of my cage. I didn't want her to know that I hadn't been walked today. Sometimes the shelter keepers get too busy and I didn't want her to think poorly of them.

As she read my kennel card I hoped that she wouldn't feel sad about my past. I only have the future to look forward to and want to make a difference in someone's life.

She got down on her knees and made little kissy sounds at me. I shoved my shoulder and side of my head up against the bars to comfort her.

Gentle fingertips caressed my neck; she was desperate for companionship.

A tear fell down her cheek and I raised my paw to assure her that all would be well.

Soon my kennel door opened and her smile was so bright that I instantly jumped into her arms. I would promise to keep her safe. I would promise to always be by her side.

I would promise to do everything I could to see that radiant smile and sparkle in her eyes. I was so fortunate that she came down my corridor. So many more are out there who haven't walked the corridors. So many more to be saved. At least I could save one.

I rescued a human today.

©2014 Rescue Me Dog; www.rescuemedog.org Janine Allen CPDT, is Rescue Me Dog's professional dog trainer. Janine's passion is working with people and their dogs. She provides demonstrations for those who have adopted shelter dogs, lends email support to adopted dog owners that need information and aids shelter staff and volunteers in understanding dog behavior to increase their adoptability.

MIKE ALMA

The Buffalo

As old as I am,
I can remember nothing else,
But it wasn't always like this.

As bold as I was,
I could never challenge them …

Their long, silver-barrelled sticks –
Spurting fire –
Left us painting the plains,
In our blood –
Many thousand bodies
Lying still as the rocks,
While many more
Uselessly paw the sky –
A sky that turns red
Behind their fading eyes …

Cloven hooves
No longer raising the dust
In storms immense …

No more watching horizons disappear –
Sunset fading before the sun, itself,
Goes down,
The herd roaming where it will,
Way beyond horizons,
Of choice …

Soon, there won't even be one,
As old as I, to remember
The tales of our magnificence …

It wasn't always like this –

Tribal Country

Go into the country,
Far from others of your kind,
And sit you down
On a crackling gold carpet.
Have great care
Not to disturb those
Who are there, before you,
For they will be there
Long after you have departed.

Choose a day of intense heat,
For it is only then, perhaps,
That you will centre in the earth,
As the sun and the heavy silence
Reduces your sight
And opens your mind
To the presence
Of life around you.
Permit the irrelevance
Of words to die –
The extravagance
Of thoughts to fade –
And watch
As the heat-haze
Envelopes you,
Taking away your range
Of vision –
The meadows around
Recede, through planes
Of heat …
Till you are alone.

Know, then,
Your insignificance
And your temporality –
Realise your place

In the history of this land –
This land that has permitted
Your birth
And supported
Your very existence.
Know your importance
And remember it well!

Morning Cloak

Nymphalis Antiopa –
Oh, Morning Cloak,
I mourn for you
And yearn for you,
But I know,
Butterfly–child
You were not created
Only to be kept
Pinned to some cork life,
For freedom is coursing
Through your being,
Pumping your blood
With tomorrow's sunshine
And, made for sun and summer,
You will find it, somewhere.

You, most beautiful of life,
Splashed with unknown
Colours of creation –
Your patterns conceived
In another world from mine,
And yet, you rested
Your silent flight
For a few brief moments
In the palm of my life,
And I thank you
For that golden time,

For it has filled me with
A gentleness I never knew,

And should I cry for you,
When you've gone,
Please forgive my child's eyes
And my child's mind,
But know, with kindness,
My tears do not regret
That you came …
Only that you passed from me
So very quickly.

Summers of a child
Are so very short
And you were such a summer
To remember …
I'm glad – so glad – you came,
Granting me your moments
With, somehow, just a little fear,
But you need not fear me,
For I would not crush you,
Or your memory,
In the closed fist
Of my loneliness …

I would not harm you
Papillion.

Rainbow Butterfly

Kahukura . . .
Sound it softly,
And feel it . . .
But gently.

Kahukura,

The Rainbow Butterfly —
Is it not as it sounds?
Is it not as it is?

Kahukura,
A silk-coloured word,
Painted by sunshine
And diamond raindrops,
Created in the sky of dreams,
Way beyond my reach,
But in my sight
And in my mind

Reach out,
To touch the rainbow,
And find it never there,
But there it is
For those who wish to see . . .
And know it.
You are the sunshine
And I wish you sun.
From the rain —
Rain from my eyes —
Pools
Splashed softly with love . . .
And I wish you love.

Without the sun
Tears are just tears —
Salt and silliness
And nothing more
When they have gone
To damp the dust . . .

Sun, should you want a rainbow . . .

Kahukura
And sound it softly.

JUDE ASHWORTH

How I Got the Native North American Indian Name of Star Turtle

She stands before you naked as the day she was born
Welcomes you, challenges you.
Challenges herself to go out and meet you
To embrace you though fear is in her heart
Fear of the unknown, the darkness and the light
She prays for her soul and moves into its very core
On a collision course of the big bang in her life
"What is out there?" she asks herself

The future is illusion dressed in perception and deception
Tenacious and frustrating as it ebbs and flows
Within her grasp teasing and torturing.
Her heart mourns for the past and embraces the future
It is beating hard in anticipation of the new.
Her mind races with thoughts and ideas
Saying 'yes' to some and chuckling at others,
Looking into the future in the eye of the storm
As thunder crashes and lightning flashes, shaking the ground.
And the wilderness in the thick of this night
High above the keening of the wind an eerie bellow of a stag is heard
She shivers and shudders as the energy pulsates around her
Stirring the air, blowing the wind like a tempest in the night.
Again she looks the future in the eye and shouts back
"What is it you have for me? Where are you taking me?"
Darkness surrounds her, envelopes her as it closes in on her
She stands firm, not flinching as the storm rattles and screams
The wind tearing at her skin in her nakedness
A waning moon emerges through the inky blackness
Reflecting light on scudding clouds
With thousands of luminous stars creating magical art to observe
This Heavenly sight takes the breath away
As a Star Turtle appears in the sky.

It Is With Regret

It is with regret
That the human race has no respect
Not for themselves, others or animals
Slavery and abuse takes place world-wide and is rife
And factory farming takes a hold
Compromising quality of life for bovine beasts
That countries we trade with have no respect
That animals in China are skinned alive
For arrogant international fur fashions

It is with regret
That fashion models and others
Parade and flaunt real fur products
They have no shame
And take no blame

Pictures of these atrocities
Can be viewed on websites
Dogs in their fear skinned alive
Blood congeals, clogs up eyelashes
For all to witness and to see
Their eyes full of pain and anguish
As they are thrown aside and left to die

It is with regret
We trade with these countries
Because we want cheap commodities
People in authority are so willing
To accept their money and not intervene

I leave you to follow through
And decide what you can do;
To pressurize those in power
To push for caveats in future projects,
To stop this degrading butchery
innocent animals suffering such cruelty.

DAVID BARBER

Lost World

If I do not do as they say
I will earn their contempt
and be beaten or worse.
They return while I am sleeping,
rapping on the bars that hold me
with their blunt persuaders.
Shattering the fine crystal of my dreams
where I race like the wind
through the forest of the night
in the spirit of a Tiger
with my eyes burning bright.
For I am lost from my world
beneath a canvas sky,
looking through these bars
'till the day I die.........

An Elephant Never Forgets

I am an orphan Elephant child,
they found me wandering in the wild.
alone, confused and terrified.
I was with my mother when she died.
She fell, ripped the air with a roar
shuddered a sigh and was no more.
They took from me with rifle gun
the one who sheltered me from sun,
who guarded me with all her might,

and kept me safe all through the night,
my earth mother my guiding light.
Then they came, in plundering cries
with white gold gleam, in frenzied eyes,
I ran and hid and watched afraid
and saw the wielding, flash of blade
cut her deep, wide open flayed.
They left her there, for those that fly
encircling above in the sky,
left me there lost, wandering wild
a helpless lone Elephant child.
But kind ones came and found me there,
who kept me safe and gave me care.
I'm still afraid, can't quite trust yet,
the past haunts me, I can't forget.

The Fate of the Wild Mammals

How cruel they be, to those born free
they hunt and kill so heinously.
A Gorilla today was sold as meat
they cut off his head, hands and feet
no more, his chest, those fists will beat.
How little they care, little they know
of God's wonder and his dire woe.
So base, so vile, this devil's spawn
when Rhinos die on an African dawn,
savagely slaughtered for their horn.
And the Elephants' plight by the white gold trade,
for the macabre art of the carvers blade.
The ignoble past has bitter recalls,
safari hunting for the trophy walls.
And whaling ships on killing sprees
with harpoon guns, on crimson seas.
And upon those left, the poacher preys

as we head towards their end of days.

WILLIAM BLAKE

The Tyger

Tyger! Tyger! burning bright
In the forests of the night,
What immortal hand or eye
Could frame thy fearful symmetry?

In what distant deeps or skies
Burnt the fire of thine eyes?
On what wings dare he aspire?
What the hand, dare seize the fire?

And what shoulder, & what art,
Could twist the sinews of thy heart?
And when thy heart began to beat,
What dread hand? & what dread feet?

What the hammer? what the chain?
In what furnace was thy brain?
What the anvil? what dread grasp
Dare its deadly terrors clasp?

When the stars threw down their spears,
And water'd heaven with their tears,
Did he smile his work to see?
Did he who made the Lamb make thee?

Tyger! Tyger! burning bright
In the forests of the night,
What immortal hand or eye
Dare frame thy fearful symmetry?

ELIZABETH BARRETT BROWNING

To Flush, My Dog

Yet, my pretty sportive friend,
Little is't to such an end
That I praise thy rareness!
Other dogs may be thy peers
Haply in these drooping ears,
And this glossy fairness.

But of thee it shall be said,
This dog watched beside a bed
Day and night unweary—
Watched within a curtained room,
Where no sunbeam brake the gloom
Round the sick and dreary.

Roses, gathered for a vase,
In that chamber died apace,
Beam and breeze resigning.
This dog only, waited on,
Knowing that when light is gone
Love remains for shining.

Other dogs in thymy dew

Tracked the hares, and followed through
Sunny moor or meadow.
This dog only, crept and crept
Next a languid cheek that slept,
Sharing in the shadow.

Other dogs of loyal cheer
Bounded at the whistle clear,
Up the woodside hieing.
This dog only, watched in reach
Of a faintly uttered speech,
Or a louder sighing.

And if one or two quick tears
Dropped upon his glossy ears,
Or a sigh came double—
Up he sprang in eager haste,
Fawning, fondling, breathing fast,
In a tender trouble.

And this dog was satisfied
If a pale thin hand would glide
Down his dewlaps sloping—
Which he pushed his nose within,
After—platforming his chin
On the palm left open.

GEORGE GORDON LORD BYRON

Epitaph to a Dog

Near this Spot
are deposited the Remains of one
who possessed Beauty without Vanity,
Strength without Insolence,
Courage without Ferocity,
and all the virtues of Man without his Vices.

This praise, which would be unmeaning Flattery
if inscribed over human Ashes,
is but a just tribute to the Memory of
BOATSWAIN, a DOG,
who was born in Newfoundland May 1803
and died at Newstead Nov. 18, 1808.

When some proud Son of Man returns to Earth,
Unknown to Glory, but upheld by Birth,
The sculptor's art exhausts the pomp of woe,
And storied urns record who rests below.
When all is done, upon the Tomb is seen,
Not what he was, but what he should have been.
But the poor Dog, in life the firmest friend,
The first to welcome, foremost to defend,
Whose honest heart is still his Master's own,
Who labours, fights, lives, breathes for him alone,
Unhonoured falls, unnoticed all his worth,
Denied in heaven the Soul he held on earth –
While man, vain insect! hopes to be forgiven,
And claims himself a sole exclusive heaven.

Oh man! thou feeble tenant of an hour,
Debased by slavery, or corrupt by power –
Who knows thee well must quit thee with disgust,

Degraded mass of animated dust!
Thy love is lust, thy friendship all a cheat,
Thy tongue hypocrisy, thy heart deceit!
By nature vile, ennobled but by name,
Each kindred brute might bid thee blush for shame.
Ye, who behold perchance this simple urn,
Pass on – it honours none you wish to mourn.
To mark a friend's remains these stones arise;
I never knew but one – and here **he lies.**

Also sometimes referred to as 'Inscription on the Monument to a Newfoundland Dog' this poem written in 1808 in honour of Lord Byron's Newfoundland dog, Boatswain, who had just died of rabies. When Boatswain contracted the disease, Byron reportedly nursed him without any fear of becoming bitten and infected. The poem is inscribed on Boatswain's tomb, which is larger than Byron's, at Newstead Abbey, Byron's estate.

The opening lines, long thought to have been written by Byron, were found to have been written by his friend John Hobhouse. Byron had originally planned to use just the last two lines as the inscription.

DAVID CALCUTT

In The Cave Of Lions

You must go deep

You must go by way of river and rockface
Squeezing yourself through the earth's eyeslit

You must go far

Where the walls dance their spirals in the flamelight
Where your shadow goes dancing before you
On the bones of the dead in the house of dreams

You must go sacred

And the gentle claws will strip away your name
Strip hair skin strip flesh from bone

You must go naked

To the utmost chamber where they wait to receive you
And their heads are not lifted they are bowed they are lowly

Two of them caressing

As your shadow dancing caresses them
And where your finger makes its mark
There the lifeblood beats
There they spring forward out of their landscape

Where the hooves drum ecstatic

Where the world roars.

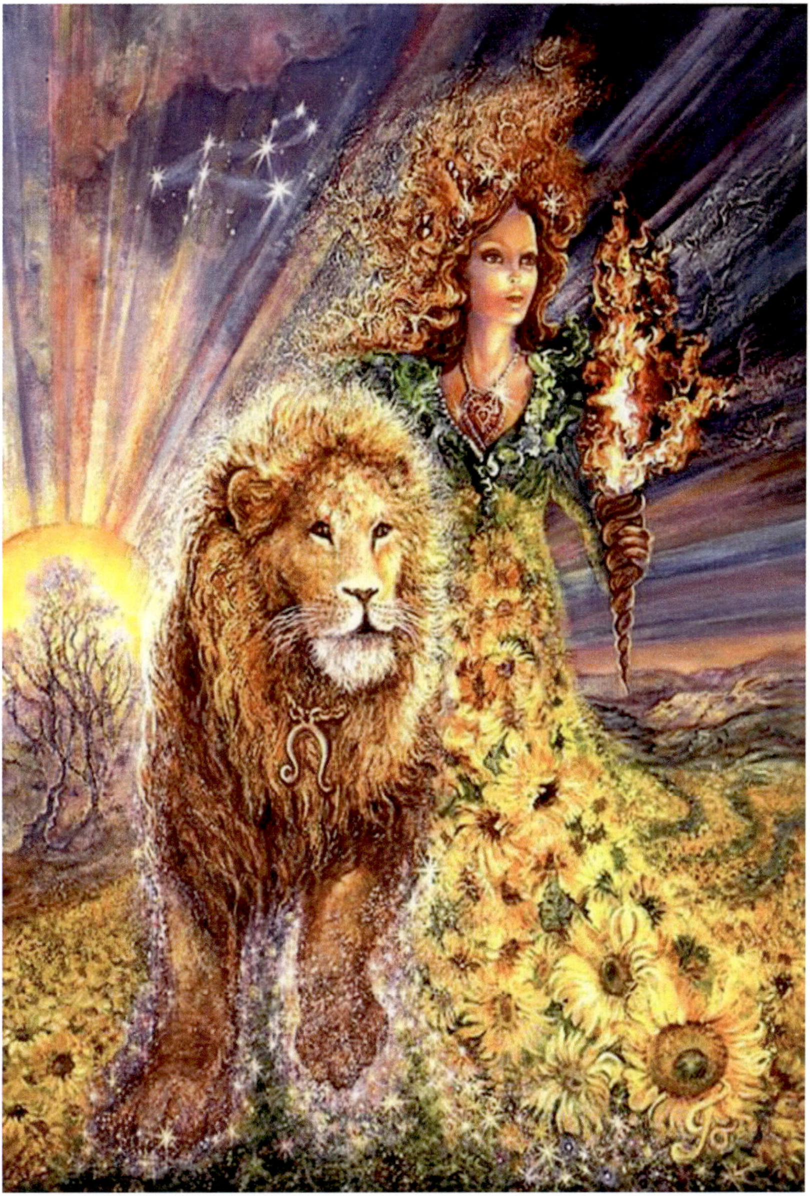

A Conjuring of the White Owl

The feather laid across my palm

A blade of light shaved from the moon
The ridged and rippled wavetop from the moon's
Frozen ocean
Where the dead sing
Weightless
Their cold high songs
That thread the ear with a needle of bone.

The stroke of finger will set it flying

A skimmed whisper across the windscreen
A ghost passing
Tree shadow to tree shadow
Making this sudden apparition
As if conjured from a crumpling of fading light,
With a cry too high
For the ear's cup to catch
Slicing the glass
Slicing the brain
A diamond clawtrack that opens the soul
To flee in its wake
To flutter

To fall.

Little orphan at the roadside
Little bundle of heat
So soft, so lightweight

Its curled feet
Left to me to cradle in its twilight dying
Stunned by its head-on collision with the world
Watching the eyes film
The gold glaze and dull
Watching the shutters come down
On a gaze straight through to the depths of space.

Where the new moon rises

Where the white owl sings.

HELEN CALCUTT

October

The sky has that blue
like bells just after ringing
the air is the cool print of a fox after it runs and leaves a memory there.
Slowly, un-wilfully, the leaves surprise.
Clocks, and tears
collecting like dead insects over the yew-burrs.
Nothing is the sadness of the tightening bark
like heat round a word
saying one thing but meaning quite another,
my love
Above the old red of the sun is hanging
her bell for the wine
and cork.

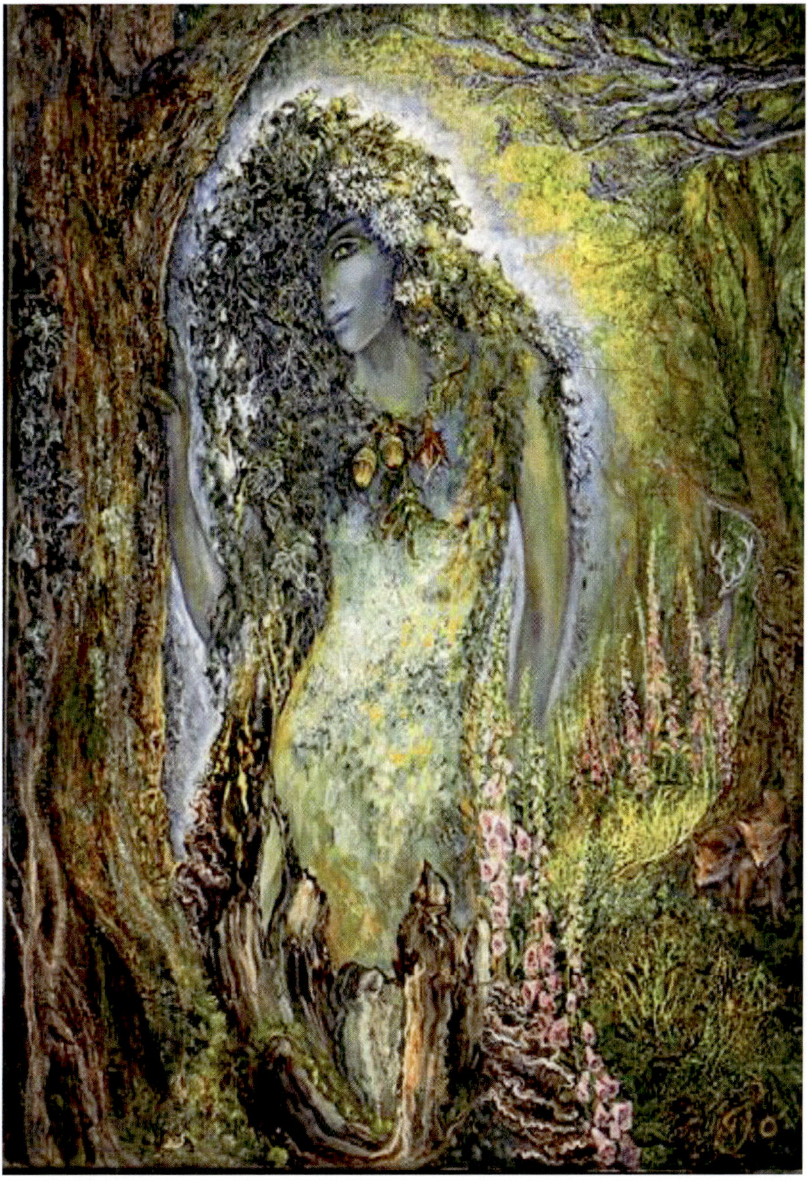

In the falling deer's mouth

There was an axe, and it buried the tree.
A footprint like God entered the blank space.

Every creaking sound was a leaking of butterflies
ring by ring, surfacing the wound. Yellow, spirit like.

A cry has taken refuge in the rock. Even now it tries
like an ache to forget itself, and be silent. Absolutely.

Where the echo runs, a lighthouse of birdsong
collapses.

G K CHESTERTON

The Donkey

When fishes flew and forests walked
And figs grew upon thorn,
Some moment when the moon was blood
Then surely I was born.

With monstrous head and sickening cry
And ears like errant wings,
The devil's walking parody
On all four-footed things.

The tattered outlaw of the earth,
Of ancient crooked will;
Starve, scourge, deride me: I am dumb,
I keep my secret still.

Fools! For I also had my hour;
One far fierce hour and sweet:
There was a shout about my ears,
And palms before my feet.

CHYI YU

DONDE VOY

All Alone I Have Started My Journey
To The Darkness Of Darkness I Go
With A Reason, I Stopped For A Moment
IN This World Full Of Pleasure So Frail
Town After Town On I Travel
Pass Through Faces I Know And Know Not
Like A Bird In Flight, Sometimes I Topple
Time And Time Again, Just Farewells
Donde Voy, Donde Voy
Day By Day, My Story Unfolds
Solo Estoy, Solo Estoy
All Alone As The Day I Was Born
Till Your Eyes Rest In Mine, I Shall Wander
No More Darkness I Know And Know Not
For Your Sweetness I Traded My Freedom
Not Knowing A Farewell Awaits
You Know, Hearts Can Be Repeatedly Broken
Making Room For The Harrows To Come
Along With My Sorrows I Buried
My Tears, My Smiles, Your Name
Donde Voy, Donde Voy
Songs Of Love tales I Sing Of No More
Solo Estoy, Solo Estoy
Once Again with My Shadows I Roam
Donde Voy, Donde Voy
All Alone As The Day I Was Born
Solo Estoy, Solo Estoy
Still Alone with My Shadows I Roam

Donde Voy ...in memory of the dogs slaughtered in Chinese cull (a song from a website that is no longer accessible) and all those victims whose only "crime" was to be a stray. (Animal Liberation Front))

ELAINE CATHERINE CHRISTIE

LEOPARDS: The Legacy of the Invisible Tribe

Through the spiralling red mists of a dust storm
A coppery-gold and black feline emerged.
Sleek, speckled with ethereal kisses,
An elegant shape-shifter with 99 inner eyes.
Freckle-faced, touched by a wizard's wand,
Instilled with spiritual knowledge
A unique instinct and an illusionist's cape,
So she can slip like a spirit between worlds.
She is the music of nature,
A Phoenix reinventing herself
Through time.

Emerald boughs cradle the tree-cat,
Her golden contours ripple like a mirage
As she sleeps safely cushioned in Thalia's wings.
In the nearness of evening she rouses,
Patiently holding her hunger,
Until light drifts and dies.
In murky fleets, eyes blaze
In a whirlwind, she shazzans the veil of life
From her prey's eyes,
Spring-boarding it weightlessly through her tree camp.

Leopards are rare relics roaming largely unnoticed,
Fearing mankind, for they have been sought after
Considered as vermin they have been burnt alive.
Despite their perseverance, her story is withering.

The Leopard is a legend and when a legend dies,
Dreams end.

*Once the Leopard was the largest land species covering half the world, more than all the other cats put together. Today only around 14 Amur Leopards remain and their enemies outnumber them 20 to 1.
Many cubs don't make adulthood and die a violent death.*

Fraying

Oracles of incense smother brushlands below
Where tribesmen have worn paths
that we have journeyed centuries before.
We are the spirits of the dead.
In the red dust sun, we have sat
cross-legged in arcane meditation.
We have tiptoed fraying air
to chase honey-dew cicadas.
Silver sashes ringing bell-tower trees,
our dark monocles highlight
our neon gaze, gargoyle-like.
Stunned as a blowpipe bleeds a threadbare future
into secret portholes of extinction.
We are the spirits of the dead –
we lie in the red dust sun in deep meditation.

Ring-tailed Lemurs are only found in Madagascar and are highly endangered. 'Lemur' means – 'spirits of the dead'

The Tiger's Tale

I
I came finally to the extreme forest
To see the secluded Emperor of fire.
His copper contours cooled beneath the surf
As he weaved and waded among river reeds,
Emerging on sweeping sands a fluid masterpiece,
An impressive frame with golden orbs that flashed.

A superlative image, mirrored in the sovereign's son,
Who strode through quaking foliage
Like a chestnut steed with wings.
Together avidly they feasted on fresh fish
Then, lazily dozed after their fill.
Their burnished honey robes, flattered by the sun.

II
"Father, who are these Titans that torment our terrain,
Baring teeth, and leering maliciously, with rods of iron?"
The Emperor sighed some wordless sorrow, then said,
"Before the Ark, before time began
We ruled every corner, before the Titan.
Now our ancestors' lights have long gone out.
They have ignored our calls, our pleas, our shouts,
Many dropped like rag dolls in crimson seas
Stripping our hides for ghoulish commodities.

I see no gilded faces in forests of green,
It is like our race have never been.
There are no granite headstones, to remember our dead,
No tears, or loving words, nor prayers be said.
So live fast my son, be all that you can be,
Death waits, in the date-less night, unforgivingly.

But there will be a reckoning, of our races wronged,
And returning, rule again the land where we belonged.

Headline: The Lion King; 20 years of roaring success

The papers say, for years fans have been thrilled again and again
at Disney's The Lion King.
Yet in Africa lion numbers have dwindled so severely,
they may be eradicated in just ten years.
Strange that they care more for a hand drawing a squiggle,
The moving finger that never caught their true majesty and beauty.

People fell in love with a sketch, a cartoon
The stardust and fakery of Hollywood,
Tinsel town's technicolor tomfoolery.
The puppeteers painted dummy,

An exuberant animation.

What influence or message do they take from this?
None that I can see,
There is no nobility, integrity or a conservation vision.
What the hand has learned -
Is to flog it for all it's worth,
And perhaps another bogglingly bright computer simulation,
Another sickly sweet illusion
will bring in big bucks
And delight its clapperboard audience,
But will do nothing for lions.

Caught in the Crossfire

I am in every war wheel and battle nest
In the mutilated misery, of shrapnel stung horses
Or the vapours of broken elephants on land mines,
In the bloody bales of dolphins and sea lions, bursting from ocean charges.
I am the expendable, weft into shrouds.

I'm in the soaking smog, of a blistering plague,
In an orphans shrill tears, as he pulls his mother's arm
Raven eyed she gawps into an abyss.
I'm in the thread bare corpses, damson draperies
Of death carved atrocities.

In the plumes of man's best friend, loyalty traded for barking bombs.
In a mother's buckling, at a grey masked glyph
That was once her son.
In the hushed pendulum for the nameless lost
I am the expendable, weft into shrouds,
I am indifference.

EMILY DICKINSON

There's a certain Slant of light

There's a certain Slant of light,
Winter Afternoons –
That oppresses, like the Heft
Of Cathedral Tunes –

Heavenly Hurt, it gives us –
We can find no scar,
But internal difference,
Where the Meanings, are –

None may teach it – Any –
'Tis the Seal Despair –
An imperial affliction
Sent us of the Air –

When it comes, the Landscape listens –
Shadows – hold their breath –
When it goes, 'tis like the Distance
On the look of Death –

I measure every Grief I meet

I measure every Grief I meet
With narrow, probing, eyes –
I wonder if It weighs like Mine –
Or has an Easier size.

I wonder if They bore it long –

Or did it just begin –
I could not tell the Date of Mine –
It feels so old a pain –

I wonder if it hurts to live –
And if They have to try –
And whether – could They choose between –
It would not be – to die –

I note that Some – gone patient long –
At length, renew their smile –
An imitation of a Light
That has so little Oil –

I wonder if when Years have piled –
Some Thousands – on the Harm –
That hurt them early – such a lapse
Could give them any Balm –

Or would they go on aching still
Through Centuries of Nerve –
Enlightened to a larger Pain –
In Contrast with the Love –

The Grieved – are many – I am told –
There is the various Cause –
Death – is but one – and comes but once –
And only nails the eyes –

There's Grief of Want – and grief of Cold –
A sort they call "Despair" –
There's Banishment from native Eyes –
In sight of Native Air –

And though I may not guess the kind –
Correctly – yet to me
A piercing Comfort it affords
In passing Calvary –

To note the fashions – of the Cross –
And how they're mostly worn –
Still fascinated to presume
That Some – are like my own –

Heaven

"Heaven" has different Signs—to me—
Sometimes, I think that Noon
Is but a symbol of the Place—
And when again, at Dawn,

A mighty look runs round the World
And settles in the Hills—
An Awe if it should be like that
Upon the Ignorance steals—

The Orchard, when the Sun is on—
The Triumph of the Birds
When they together Victory make—
Some Carnivals of Clouds—

The Rapture of a finished Day—
Returning to the West—
All these—remind us of the place
That Men call "paradise"—

Itself be fairer—we suppose—
But how Ourself, shall be
Adorned, for a Superior Grace—
Not yet, our eyes can see—

DES – LONE WOLF

A Wolf's Plea

As I walk alone into the night,
Scared and lonely with no more fight.
I try to think of what is was that made them hate me so,
Somebody out there please hear my cries,
I'm tired and lonely. I don't want to die.
I am lost and wondering with no place left to go,
My loved ones were taken down below.
The shadows of wings came flying over above,
I had turned my head to see nothing but blood.
Nothing for me to do but run,
Oh, how they had taken the ones I love.
I hide behind a tree,
Hoping they won't see me.
Trying to catch my breath,
All I hear is death.
Why have they forsaken me,
Taking our souls and our dignity.
I run away as far as I can,
Knowing tomorrow there will be Wings landing again.
So if you hear my cries across the skies,
Please ask them for me. Why?
And when they look at you with a grin,
With an answer that makes no sense.
Please tell them for me,
That I now too have wings to fly.

Please pass this on to enlighten those oblivious to the plight of the great and wonderful wolves of Alaska!
Des (A LONE WOLF) Animal Liberation Front

EUGENE EGAN

The Captive Primate

I look out of this cage
With a sense of rage
They stop and stare
Filling me with despair

Dark and angry
Torment withers inside me
Captive enclosure keeps me here
A living death through stealth

Barren existence
Grinding me down
Torment persists without end
My spirit burning away

Yearning to be free
To roam again
Without pain
And not for others' gain

I stare beyond the confines of this cage
Loam and metal is my miserable stage
Can you see the sorrow behind my eyes?
Torn from forests and kinfolk ties.

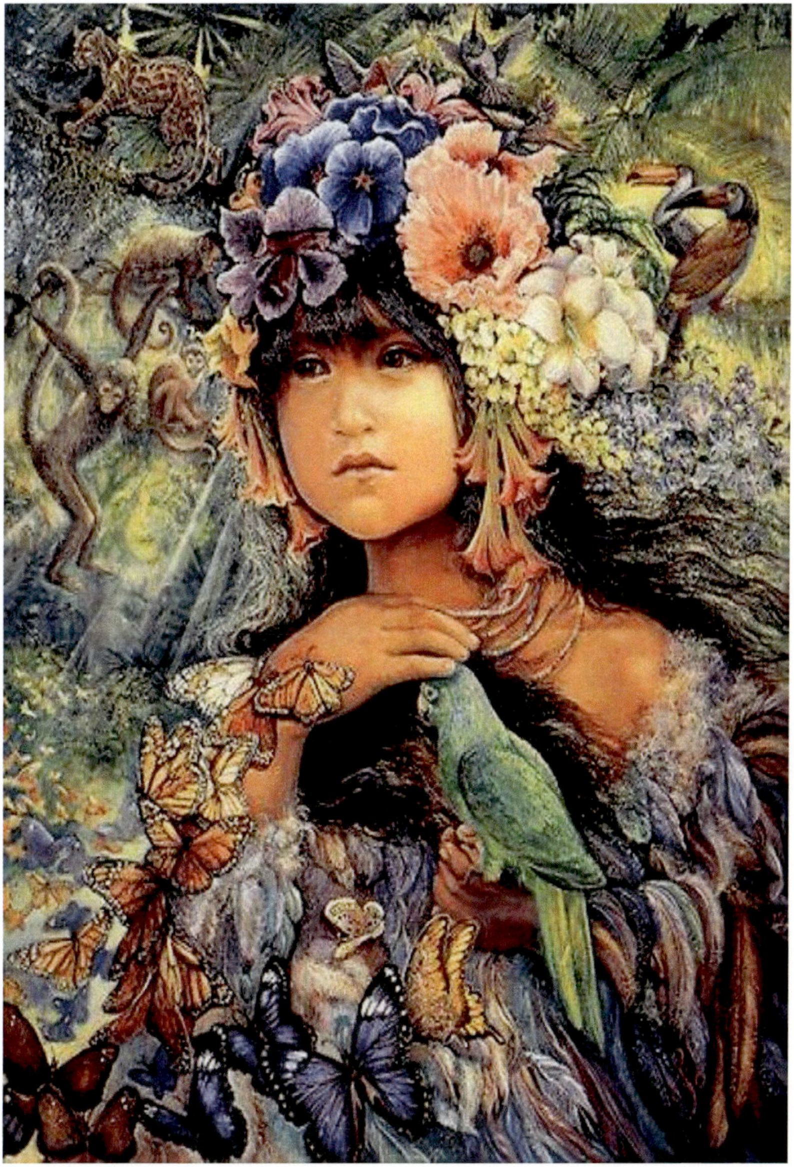

The Elephant

Born to run free and wild
Ever since she was a child
Till one day doom and gloom
Came upon the elephant in the room

Mankind trekked into her world
Closed down the light
And opened a heart of darkness
An inferno came to be

Spreading fear without a tear
Rape and pillage was their game
Murder sanitised for profit of ivory
Genocide and extinction

The elephant in the room
Will one day no longer be
The ivory business thrives
As she slowly dies.

GIOVANNI SPOZ ESPOSITO

There's No Leopard Like Snow Leopard

When I was five,
A while ago,
A man on the telly said
"Snow... leopard in jeopardy"
I said "Mom can I go…?
To jeopardy, to see the snow leopard-y?"
"No" said Mom "You've misunderstood
In jeopardy means 'danger',
It doesn't sound good
For the snow leopard- in jeopardy."
"But why's he in danger?
Is he crossing the road?
Hasn't he learnt to do the green cross code?
He needs his own crossing,
Like a zebra or pelican,
We need to tell people,
Like the man on the telly can."
"No dear," said Mom "it's a bit worse than that,
The future looks bleak for the big snowy cat.
It's out of our hands.
There's not much we can do."
But now you know
And I know
That just isn't true.
Sometimes moms will say things
To keep us kids at bay.
Snow leopard-y in jeopardy?
We can change that today.

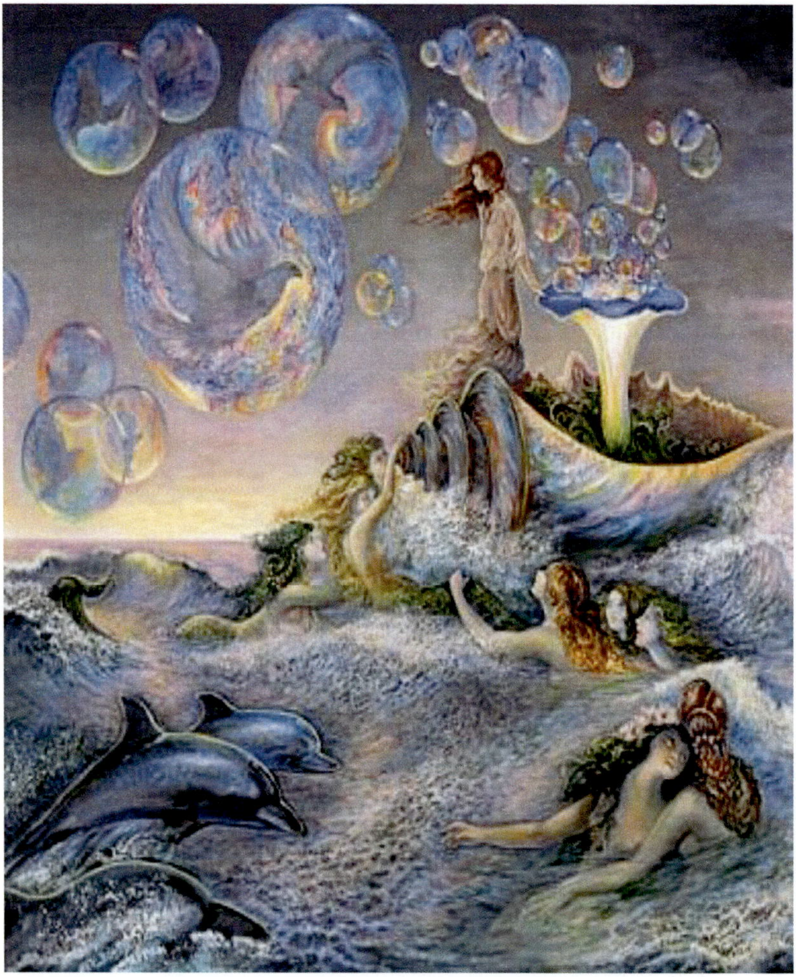

Dolphin Bubble

Dolphin bubble,
Belly dancing,
All the way to the top,
When it breaks the ocean surface,
It's going to go 'pop'.
When it breaks the ocean surface,
It's going to make a noise,
Like the one the dolphin made
With all the dolphin girls and boys;
At the school
Where all the dolphins go,
Where they're taught,
"It's not the size of bubble you blow,
Just so long as
You're forever blowing bubbles,
And your bubbles
Don't cause trouble,
But leave a ripple".

CHRIS FEWINGS

Warmth

I take the perfect white-furred skin
and nail it to my wall, paw by paw.
Opposite, an exploration map stretched tight,
flags marking our advance.

The last bear in the wild. Still,
the DNA is bottled, and we've paid Saami
to manage a safari park. Who knows?
They might return.

Ice. It got in the way. The world needs oil.
I do my job. The economy is growing.
They say the globe is warming.
Nothing's proven.

I shot her myself. Put her out of her misery.
Greenpeace wanted to keep her on her floe,
starving, for publicity. A colleague adopted the cub.
We care.

Girlfriend wanted her for a coat.
I got her a seal instead.
I wanted to keep a reminder of Eden
here in the field.

They're amazing, the Northern Lights.

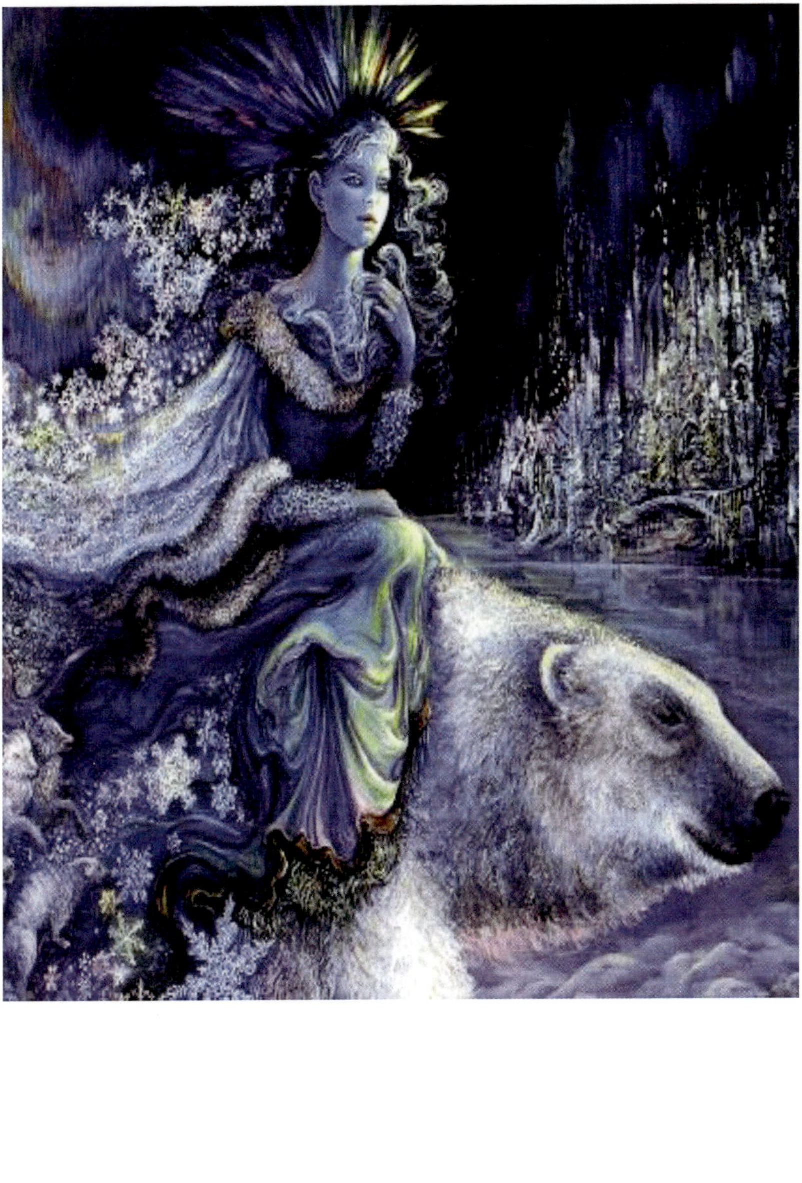

SKIN

I slip out of my skin

a second time, try on

a tiger. In my dreams.

Waking, I hunt down

mice and rats in concrete,

stroke the cat.

She sits on my lap,

purring, as I sew

a dozen skins together.

 In time, I'll have

an eiderdown. Rats' tails:

strong and long -

 I make a mobile

for my granddaughter,

tiny mammal at the teat.

CAROLINE GILL

Muffled Drum

Silence,

then the throb of pulse on stone:
stifled pangs vibrate through bars.
Pacing paws go round and round:
echoes come but no one stirs.
Jet and amber flying lizards
and their wings above the cell:
how they love their music-making,
stringing notes from wall to wall.

Midnight shadows chase the moon,
brand a stave with stripes of ink.
Muffled drum-beats sound in vain:
quavers pelt a dappled flank.
Stars retreat while ticking rhythms
rise from song sheets for the dawn.
Lizards fill their scales with freedom
while a tiger hunkers down.

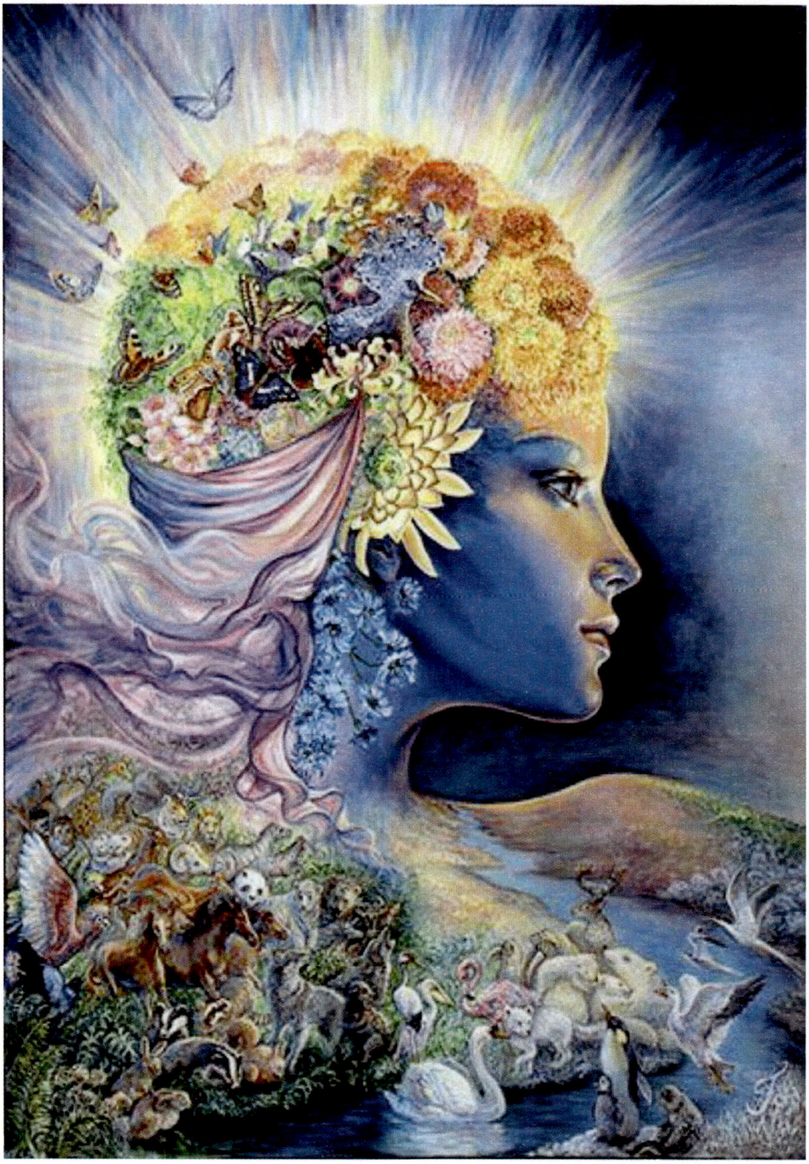

Letter from the Bush

Dear world, the time has come to share a dream
or two perhaps, for here our paths divide.
So as the minutes drift along a stream,
I'll tell you what I note on either side.
The bush is lush with water holes for all:
young rhinos paddle while their parents stand
about in rainbow light. Their kingdom's wall
is never-ending in this fertile land.
But turn and look across: dust, drought and thorn
define a tract where rhinos fail to thrive.
A single adult, lost without his horn,
ploughs through a wilderness: can he survive?
You claim to share my dream, but fail to see
that creature on the distant bank is me.

OLIVER WENDELL HOLMES

To A Caged Lion

Poor conquered monarch! though that haughty glance
Still speaks thy courage unsubdued by time,
And in the grandeur of thy sullen tread
Lives the proud spirit of thy burning clime;--
Fettered by things that shudder at thy roar,
Torn from thy pathless wilds to pace this narrow floor!

Thou wast the victor, and all nature shrunk
Before the thunders of thine awful wrath;
The steel-armed hunter viewed thee from afar,
Fearless and trackless in thy lonely path!
The famished tiger closed his flaming eye,
And crouched and panted as thy step went by!

Thou art the vanquished, and insulting man
Bars thy broad bosom as a sparrow's wing;
His nerveless arms thine iron sinews bind,
And lead in chains the desert's fallen king;
Are these the beings that have dared to twine
Their feeble threads around those limbs of thine?

So must it be; the weaker, wiser race,
That wields the tempest and that rides the sea,
Even in the stillness of thy solitude
Must teach the lesson of its power to thee;
And thou, the terror of the trembling wild,
Must bow thy savage strength, the mockery of a child!

RANGZEB HUSSAIN

Upon hearing of the death of the Monarch of the Moorlands

These mist covered mountains of the highlands,

'twas here that I once freely wandered upon natures pasture grounds,

Now I lie shrouded in the mournful fog of the lowlands,

'twas here that I was met by a pack of bone breaking hounds.

The fresh dew upon the harvest of autumn's final flowering,

'twas here that I chewed the grass of sweet nature's offering,

Now I grow cold upon the ground where I was stalked by dark doom,

'twas here that I left life's rocky way under a hunter's moon.

The air of the early morn moor with the sky above my dome,

'twas here that I ran and with joy loved and royally roamed,

Now my legs will nevermore *click* or *clack* over my domain fenced with tree gates,

'twas here that I wooed and won my shy majestic mate.

She, my queen of the green woodlands, she was my wife and my empire,

'twas here that we romanced in the fading summer's fire,

Our charming child, my princess of these grassy hills now cloaked in shade,

'twas here that she saw her father the monarch in death finally fade.

In the chorus of the dancing dawn awakening upon the horizon's golden rhyme,

'twas here that I sang the tune that will drum till the end of nature's time,

They will come with stakes and wood and cross and bow me to the beams,

'twas here where they hacked and tore off my enchanted crown of weeping dreams.

The scent of the freshly mown grass mingles with the green pine,

'twas here that I drank the perfume and nectar of the divine,

My eyes glaze, my breathing falters, my clay chills, my soul no more sings,

'twas here that I finally returned to the hands of my Beloved, the eternal King.

"...I shall now graze upon the sacred acres of my Creator,

I shall frolic and run free in the tender fields of endless splendour..."

The largest animal in Great Britain, a red stag named Emperor who stood over 9ft tall, was shot dead by a trophy hunter. The antlers of the majestic deer are highly prized, and after pictures of the stag appeared in the national press, the animal was tracked and killed in Exmoor, Devon.

The Grave of the Unknown Dog

What have I done, my master, that angers you so?

I crept into this world on an icy cold dark night,

But once you showed me warmth and light,

My father I did not see,

Father you did for a time become to me,

I still treasure those spring days happily,

It was an age when the fresh earth laughed madly

(And you men smiled with it).

Once days of light darkened

Murky red and it was my blood I saw hardened

On your hands, my father,

My master, my friend, are

You mine enemy?

In your greatest hour I did stand by you,

Mine fatal hour was at hand and I cried out for the truth,

In my beggar's voice I pleaded to you

To guard, today, my children and their generations too

As I once did yours.

I never sold or bargained my love

But you traded yours for scrap paper doves,

My eyes always glistened,

These days I weep salt tears and ask you to listen,

My idiot smile always seemed foolish but now I wear

Pagliacci's lipstick.

While you desecrate my humble gravestone

I never once did the same in spite, hate or even while digging for a bone,

I shall always play the fool

Who is used as a tool

And nothing more by you.

Where are you now? Were not you and I fashioned out from blood?

Of the same mud,

By the one God?

I never changed my tune which was composed by a bard

But I hear you dance to a different hymn,

They say Satan was Keeper of the Music Inn

Before he was sent down

To a place where he found a sound

That forever changed his jig.

I did have two eyes,

You used your blind eyes for lies,

My nose I gave up for your nightly protection

While you always smelt for election,

You have two deaf ears,

Mine always heard the sound of fears,

You once did have a heart, mine bled,

I hang my head and go to my earthen bed,

Compassion is a word that spells dread

For Humankind.

The rags that you men worship daily

Drove you to haunt me gaily,

If careful you are not

Those same rags will one day sink their needle teeth into your soft rot,

The needle that put me to into Death's sleep

Will bury into you deep indeed

And bite softly it will, like lice,

Will you howl like I did *(out of pain, not cowardice)*,

Or are you going to offer the other cheek?

I was crucified for your guilt

Which upon my shoulders you day by day built,

Mine life was extinguished under the burning weight,

Even in rigid death you hound me mate

And thousands like me are detained,

But loyal we will remain,

In the fiery jaws of hellish Death

I never spat out my love but I bet

You never wept,

My master who once did return my love.

What have I done, my master, that angers you so?

The tabloid press in Great Britain orchestrated a rabid campaign to outlaw the American Bulldog breed after a handful of reports filtered in about how some of these dogs had attacked people. The sensationalist reports were so sustained, on a systematic daily basis, that the government eventually capitulated and passed a law which not only forbade people from importing the breed into the UK but also for all American Bulldogs on British soil to be detained and destroyed. Instead of reprimanding irresponsible owners who may have abused and conditioned their dogs to be aggressive, the government issued a blanket ban on the entire breed. Thus, within weeks, an entire breed of dog was wiped clean from the shores of Great Britain. Police raided homes and snatched away family pets and exterminated them with lethal injection. For the crimes of a few the entire breed paid the penalty with their lives.

SARAH JAMES

The Hummingbird Case

Delicate beaks poised,
elegant light-strumming wings
pinned unhumming
to a broken twig frame.

A filigree of holes, this lacework
tree of feather and claws.
Distanced, death's plumage
not so brittle, so torn.

This case shimmers with dreams
spun from sun, textured
with oceans, forests, skies…
What's done is done. Yet,

even as I reach for the gleam
of these half-kiss scissor tails,
I feel silence cut.
To seize the beaks, tug them and…

my stillness snaps their wings.

This poem was first published in Magma. The nineteenth century hummingbird case is displayed in the Birds gallery of the Natural History Museum, London. Many hummingbird species are now considered endangered and threatened with extinction.

Shadow Wolves

Their soft fur – moon white, black as a dark
night, or the grizzled grey of flecked slate –

was not made for stillness or the puppet
motion of stolen sleekness draped over

human bones. Do not be surprised if
the weight of absent flesh rests heavily

on the wearer's shoulders or the skin
beneath starts to stink of rotten meat.

Death lingers in the shadowed fur.
Wild lives cannot be worn with grace

by those with no right to their beauty.

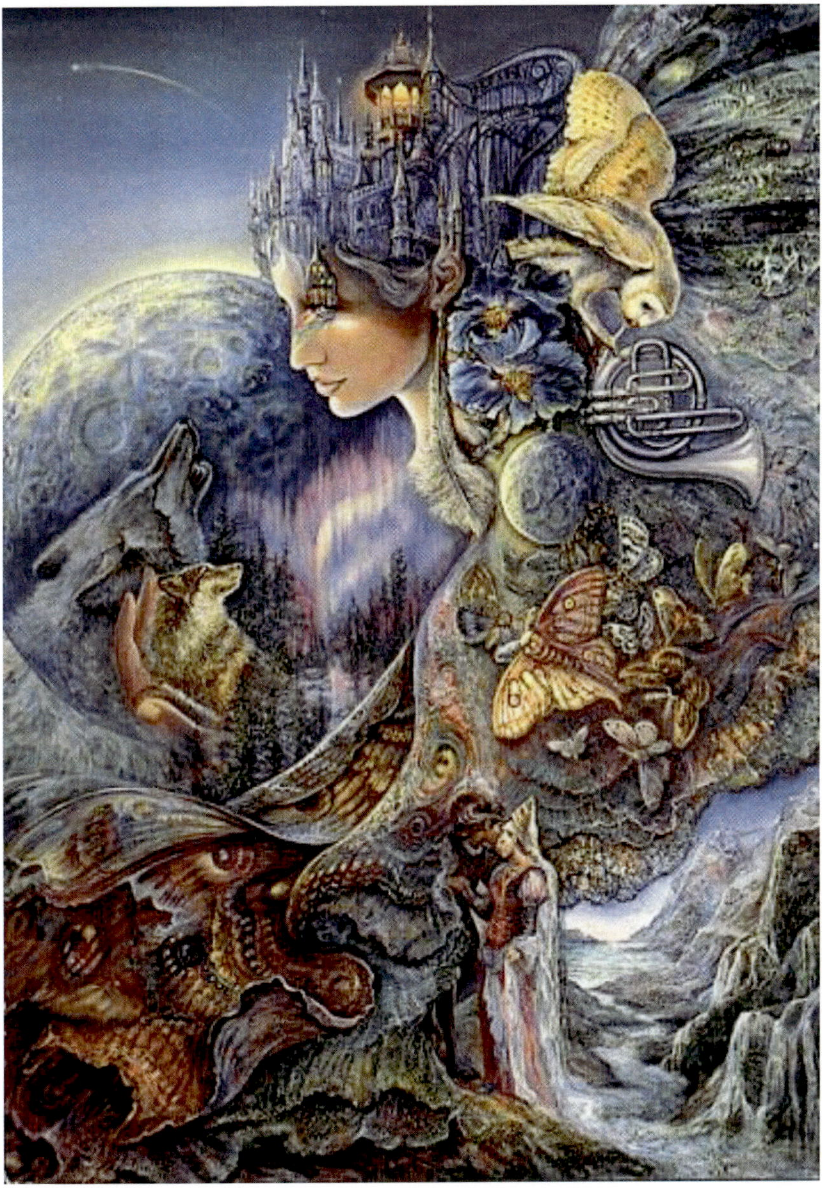

Wild Cat

The taut sloped 'j'
of his lithe body in mid-
pounce on swamp prey.

The open-mouthed 'a'
of his wide jaw crushing
a skull in one bite.

The throat-coughed 'g'
of his rainforest roar,
a paw stretched out

to fish in the curved 'u'
of a pool hidden
by pampas undulations.

The symmetric spaced 'a'
of his eyes: dark suns set
into liquid amber.

The graceful muscled 'r'
of a head held above water,
his wake sleek.

Imagine this lightning
jolt of wild beauty
reduced

to just a film repetition
or a picture fixed still on a page,
life traced out

until nothing is left
but flat images
and printed letters' black bones.

The Grey, White and Red of It

Hauled from its infinite blue ocean, slit
only by the soft arrows of flitting fish,

the lone whale shark now beached
on the factory floor. Oar-size knives

in its dotted grey back. Its belly cut
open. Guts exposed. Hacked up.

White slabs of flesh – for face creams,
lipsticks, health pills. Or for the dead

delicacy of shark fin soup. The grey
and white of its life streaked with red,

oiling the hands of those already fat
on slaughterhouse riches.

Unbound

There's a tiger in the cathedral crypt.
Echoes pace. Even padded paws sigh,
claws stiletto-tap: metres of interlocking arches
less than a sweep of its tail.

A lit match in the wild, here its stripes
are a hanging of whites, oranges and black:
a brooding shroud for the tombs.
                        But its dying eyes
still burn brighter than candles on the altar.

Do not ask him to prowl the dark like a trapped cat

burglar. He will not lie down in stillness
to whimper and lick his mossed tree-stump paws,
claws etching his days into the cracked stone floors

of those who would cage or kill his wildness
instead of their own darkness inside.
No! Let him pounce from shadow corners,
leap against oak doors, bound up the steps, push

down mans hand-built walls, break through stained glass, out to the
sunlight now untrapped from his eyes,
as he streaks across grasslands,
then weaves his flame through mangrove swamps

into the forests leafy wet denseness:
His symmetry unbound – and made for moving.

In support of the Tiger, Tiger campaign to save this endangered species

JANET JENKINS

Give Us Sweet Peace. A Tiger's Plea.

Poetry in motion, but wanted for potions;
we're a dying breed and I fear it's too late.
The evil ones came, they trapped my brother;
their only thought was exterminate!

Our body parts have special powers;
they're wanted for healing, or so I am told.
I stalk through the jungle in search of a meal,
while poachers are prowling
and waiting to steal:
my whiskers, for toothache,
my brain for spots,
my bile, for convulsions,
my testes, for nodes,
my teeth, for rabies, sores
and charms.
The list is endless my caring friends,
It's time to speak out;
support our cause.

Stop these bullies; give us sweet peace.
Fight for our beauty; protect our land.
Help us to cope in a challenging world,
Please give us a future;
it's all in your hands.

The Uninvited Guest

He's here again,
My bicolour feline friend,
playing peek-a-boo
from an earthy gap
between the Pittosporum
and the Pieris.

He meets my gaze

but remains still;
pretends to be invisible.
"Yes I know you're there"
I whisper to the air.
"But why? this isn't your home."

He glides out of the shrubbery;
a speech bubble appears above his head:
"You're not going to move me are you?"
He looks at me with appealing eyes.

He edges closer to the house
and alights on the dewy lawn,
enjoying the sun's early rays.
The bubble says,
*"I like it here
in my garden comfort zone."*

I used to shoo him away,
my black and white intruder,
but now I've warmed
towards this fleeting friend;
he takes nothing away
(not even a scrumptious sparrow)
and leaves nothing behind.

He suddenly rises and moves hastily
towards the fence
brushing past Hypericums
and Hellebores
Sedums and Skimmias.
The bubble says
*"It's time for me to leave this peaceful place;
tomorrow I'll bring a present; a mouse."*
I gasp and gulp.
and over the fence and away
and hope I misread that last bubble!

NINA LEWIS

Nerve Endings

Over the years man developed language.

Words hold power, power rules.

If only we recognized ourselves as the animals we are,

just like them,

we communicate, experience life through basic senses,

if these things happened on both sides of the line

people would stand up and take notice.

Factory farm animals slaughtered by trivia.

Pain inflicted throughout the process, horror felt.

We are not Gods. We are animals,

animals with words and moral responsibility.

Put yourself in their position,

those animals suffer by our actions.

This is reality. Don't cut yourself off,

it matters to them.

It matters to you.

At the Hands of Humans

Trusting dark eyes stare out from behind the cage

an expression of insecurity

sorrowful mistrust,

Head bowed,

the human hand persists,

voice soothes as fingers stretch out and repeat

the motions through the small opening.

Minutes later the response is love,

licking the fingers of the hand that saved him,

released him from captivity.

He and eight others are transported

sadness burning in their eyes,

a branding tattoo inside each ear,

A number.

An item.

The first moment outside captivity is

captured on film.

They have never seen the sun

Or clawed the earth

and when their cages are opened they

have no idea what to do.

Wary of life beyond the metal.

Trusting spirits still intact

with encouragement and time

they wander out to explore the world.

The same world that wrote them

a very different life story.

The Night Sky

The night sky
saved me
on occasion,
back when times
were complicated
when my world
was broken
beyond repair.

In a time,
I believed there was
no way back,
I stood silently
and looked up.

Like Narnia
I found space
in the night sky.
Saw bridges
that didn't exist
between the stars,
faith.
I allowed its
deep beauty
to clothe me,
hide me.

It promised
to watch
as I fell asleep.
Just as you do, nowadays.

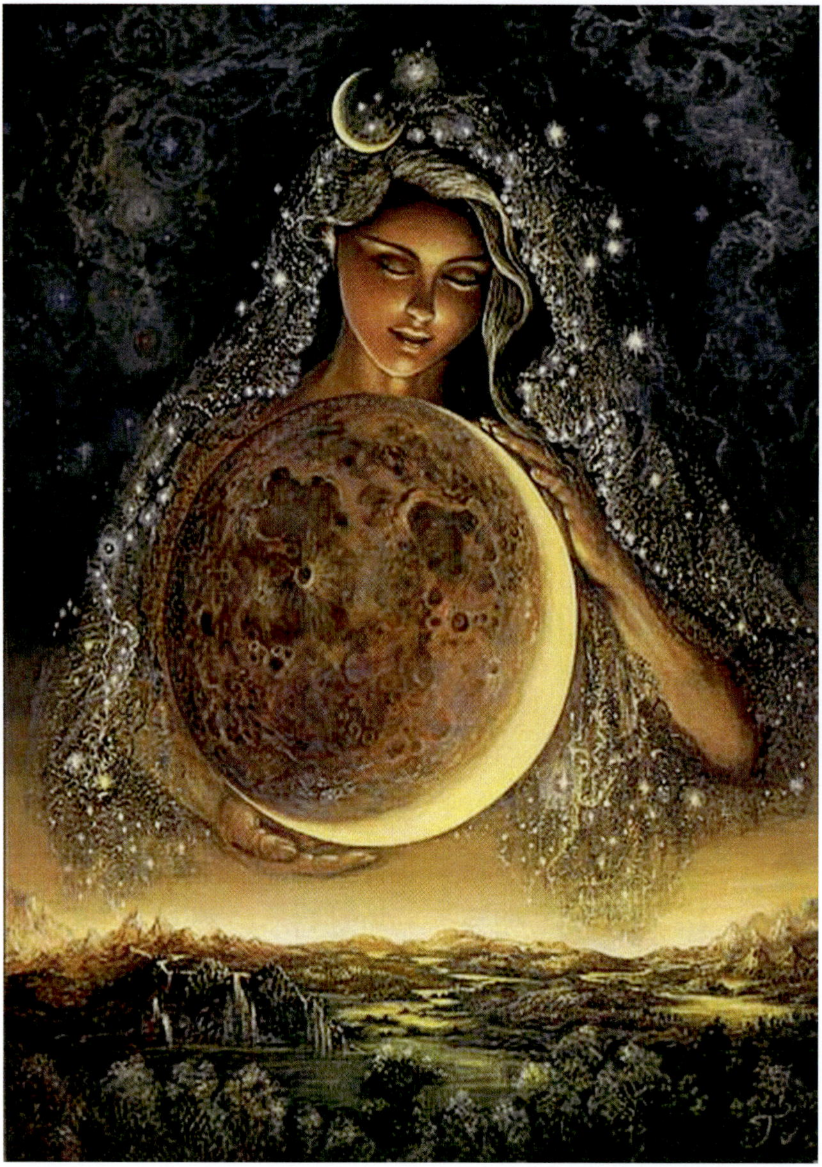

Universe

Night sky, structural complexity
looks simple when you're standing this far away.
Shallow breathing, head hinged back, it blocks my windpipe.
The same feeling I had when called to the front of class to stand close
to the chalk board, decipher an algorithm.

Out here the universe expands, yet it feels no different from the first time.
I stood less than two feet tall and looked up and up.

I cannot read stars, they look the same on this side of the equator
to my untrained eye.
Moving home from London I discover the stars again, excitement,
akin to watching screaming fireworks, amplified.

Lying on car bonnets, with a younger spine,
starring up at the night's net cast.
Now I'm discovering stars visiting us in our new garden,
beginning to spot the familiar constellations before you have chance
to name them and trace them with your finger through the air.

Just like stars, you and I mix, our lighter sides become heavier,
masked, protected, Energy pulsates invisibly between us.
Nuclear fusion.

TESSA LOWE

Spellbound

When I was a child it was Chameleons;
And Shongalulus:
I never did know how to spell
Those hard black curly creatures
With the hundred legs
Centipede is easier
Yet somehow Shangalulu stays
Camouflaged:
Unlike the strange Chameleon
Who so stunned me into silence
When I lost him, blended into the
Dappled shade of mulberry and avocado:
When I found him secreted; changed
Still; one paw or claw or footpad
Poised aloft, indecisive, I watched him
Spellbound still myself
In wonder: listening to the crickets
Scratch their incessant fiddles
Through summer's reeling days.

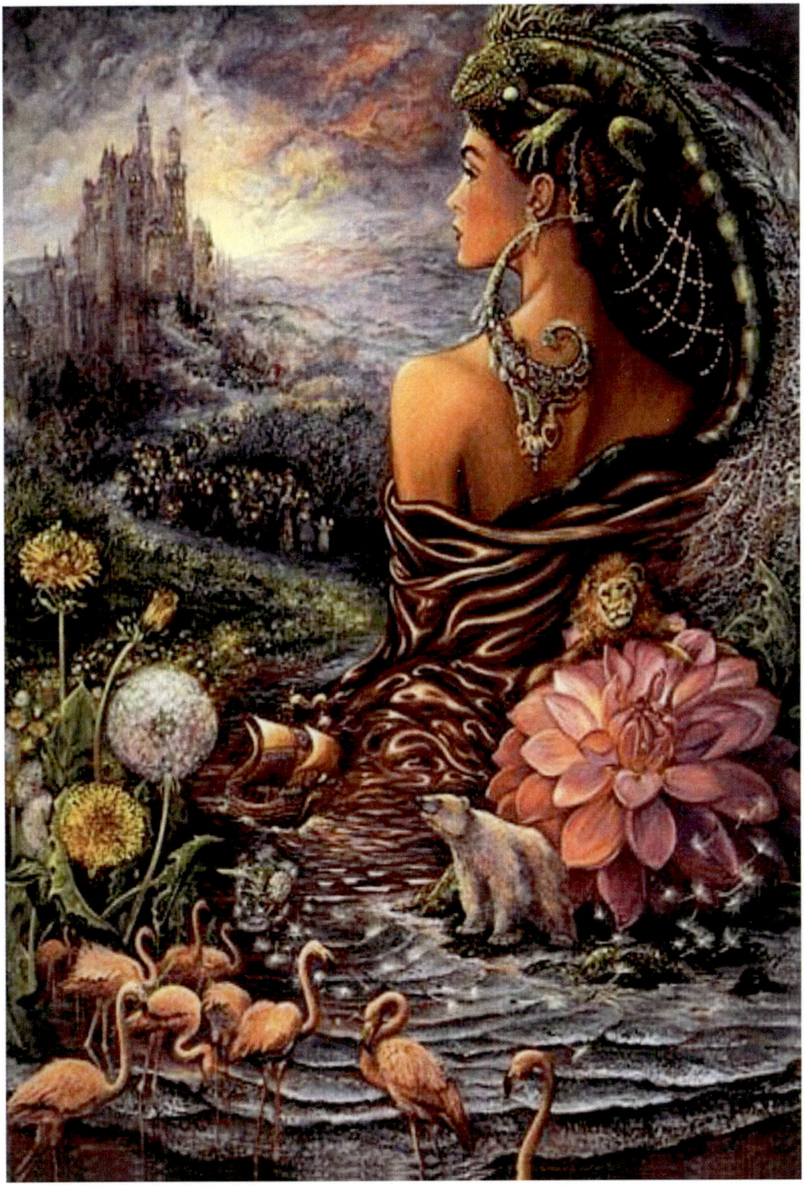

Colourful Brood

My mother always said
She should have been a farmer's wife
And had six children:
As it was, she was an actress
And had only me; I don't think
I was a disappointment but tried
Too hard I fear, to be the other five
Just to make sure.

She wasn't able to bear her
Craved for babes but made up
For not being a farmer's wife
By breeding birds;
Zebra Finches Gouldian Finches
Java sparrow's big cockatiels
And tiny quail; mallard ducks
Muscovy ducks, bantam hens
Laying hens, cocky cockerels.

Every day she would survey
Her tiny half an acre
Followed by her faithful brood:
Wire haired terrier
Long haired Persian
Budgerigar
Siamese cat and me.

CHARLOTTE MEW

The Trees Are Down

He cried with a loud voice: Hurt not the earth, neither the sea, nor the trees - Revelation

They are cutting down the great plane-trees at the end of
the gardens.
For days there has been the grate of the saw, the swish of
the branches as they fall,
The crash of the trunks, the rustle of trodden leaves,
With the 'Whoops' and the 'Whoa', the loud common talk,
the loud common laughs of the men, above it all.

I remember one evening of a long past Spring
turning in at a gate, getting out of a cart, and finding
a large dead rat in the mud of the drive.
I remember thinking: alive or dead, a rat was a
god-forsaken thing,
but at least, in May, that even a rat should be alive.

The week's work here is as good as done. There is just
one bough
on the roped bole, in the fine grey rain,
Green and high
And lonely against the sky.
(Down now! -)
And but for that,
If an old dead rat
did once, for a moment, unmake the Spring, I might never
have thought of him again.

It is not for a moment the Spring is unmade to-day;
These were great trees, it was in them from root to stem:
When the men with the 'Whoops' and the 'Whoas' have carted

the whole of the whispering loveliness away
Half the Spring, for me, will have gone with them.

It is going now, and my heart has been struck with the
hearts of the planes;
Half my life it has beat with these, in the sun, in the rains,
In the March wind, the May breeze,
In the great gales that came over to them across the roofs from the great seas.
There was only a quiet rain when they were dying;
They must have heard the sparrows flying,
And the small creeping creatures in the earth where they were lying -
But I, all day, I heard an angel crying:
'Hurt not the trees'

In The Fields

Lord when I look at lovely things which pass,
  Under old trees the shadow of young leaves
Dancing to please the wind along the grass,
  Or the gold stillness of the August sun
 on the August sheaves;
Can I believe there is a heavenlier world than this?
  And if there is
Will the heart of any everlasting thing
  Bring me these dreams that take my breath away?
They come at evening with the home-flying rooks
and the scent of hay,
Over the fields. They come in spring.

MATT NUNN

On Safari 'hubris' is the Tastiest Snack

Having tried to stalk and annihilate his reckoned-to inferior species
Because he could,
The shit once almighty him who tangled with the wrong
Mean and moody right maney hard bastard
In the heavily spoilt by him dog eat jungle
Has got no grumble grounds to whinge
Like a wrong'un banker caught
With his blunted bling grasping claws
In what is not his to rob,
But still strums the chinless equine self-pity
Of this hunter yobbo dominatrix class,
From deep within the churning burial bowels
Of his majesty the rightful true munching predator.

Revenge is not necessarily the best dish but it is at least the better one.

ANTONY OWEN

The War Dog

The boy that came of age barked Mater
send a shepherd with brandy to no man's land
pack lucky strikes with a bandage and bullet.

Watch her zig zag to the dander of wounds
to alps of caps in blood thawed snow
to the Morse code eyes of Gunther.

Watch her saunter through mangroves of khaki,
past a letter from Jenny concerned about lying
she hadn't bled since that weekend in Bristol.

Watch her limp to a crater to drink,
the black shepherd, the sea of tranquillity,
two shepherds afloat in no man's land.

The dog that came of age barked Mater,
send a sniper to end its misery

"I can't shoot a dog Sir, I just can't Sir".

Zoology

Sail the eyes of a primate
mauling apples from fenced out trees
swaying with tractor tyres.

Lions of a concrete savannah,
lap away their reservoir ghosts,
jeeps roar for them.

Protected pandas in foie-gras seraglios
chow bamboo from Dobbies World
as the world gets it on.

The lethargic cheetah is all ran out
crawling out with butchered gruel
from sponsored carrier bags.

Unlock the cages, the zoo is extinct.
The animals are toys stuffed with
manmade threads.

MALINI PATEL

Animals in 2050

There once was a place called Salem
Where girls lived deep in fear
Of being accused of witches brews
Then knowing death was near.

Another time in Georgia
When black men had no rights
They were beaten and degraded
With so many sleepless nights.

And most recently it's gay men
Who have proudly proclaimed "it's time!"
That love from man to man
Be simply not a crime.

There was a place called Auschwitz
Where Polish and Jews were gassed
It's a very sad reminder
Of how very cruel our past.

And can you believe that women
Were not allowed to read?
They could not vote or think freely
They existed merely to please.

And now the time we live in
It's just the same you see
Animals are the slaves and women
Longing to be free!

There is but just one difference
For animals have no voice.
They cannot band together

They simply have no choice!

They must follow all our orders
Die for many meals
They give their lives for research
And have no courts from which to appeal.

They are stuck inside the evil trap
of peoples compassionless views.
Animal lovers are their only hope
Of spreading this vital news....

Animals do have feelings!
They feel loneliness and pain!
We must love and respect them!
We'll all have much to gain!

So let us come together
And fight for this huge cause
For we are their last chance
To change our current laws.
Let's not waste our time on hunters
Or argue with the blind
Let's focus on the children
And educate their minds.

If we can teach compassion
as Liz C. Stanton did long ago
Then animals can have a future
And a culture of compassion can grow.

And so my friends, I leave you
With just one thought in mind
The suffering of the animals
Is caused by humankind.

Humans have a past of cruelty
As the slaves and women knew

But with time and education
Civility slowly grew.

And so I pray to heaven
That 50 years from now
Animal suffering will be non-existent
And people will look back and think HOW?

Copyright © 2000 by Malini Patel. All Rights Reserved
May be used in unchanged form by a vowed Animal Rightists.

JADE PHIPPS

Through the eyes of the Wild

As I understand it
You are the intellectuals
Self-cast as the rulers of our world
Yet I feel disregarded.
It takes some intellect to acquire
Skills to live in the wild!
You have devised certain rules
For you it is a punishment
To be locked behind bars
Then why is it
Against our will
With no trial
You decide to lock us in a cage
Punished for just being.
No regard for our feelings
You just abduct us from what we know.
Where we are happy
And put us in a cage.
You try to justify your actions
Calling it protection.
The cruelty in which my brothers
And I have received from your kind
Is unfathomable.
A mockery of our intelligence
Abolishment of free will
You make a profit from our misfortune.
You savages have the audacity
To call us beasts
Yet we have never broke into
Your homes
We have never had the gusto
To take what is not rightfully ours.
Why don't you see the pain?
In which you have inflicted?

Stop to think and listen
We did not ask you to interfere
Play God
And remove us from our homes
Stop now before it is too late.
Let us determine our own fate
Open the gates
And let us roam free
Let us return to where
We should be
No bars
No chains
Throw away the key
Let us return home
The wild
Where we can run free.

CLARE POWERS

A World for the Future:
Does it have to be like this?

The stupidities of man
The deadly consequences become clear.
Our beautiful world lost forever
Does it have to be like this?

Man's inhumanity is hard to understand,
His lust for materialism has clouded the way.
Our beautiful world lost forever
Does it have to be like this?

The long term effects not thought of
The trust betrayed for selfish desire
Our beautiful world lost forever
Does it have to be like this?

When the earth finally becomes dust
It'll be too late to change
The sadness of our of our actions irreversible
Our beautiful world lost forever
Does it have to be like this?

It doesn't have to be like this!
Let's stop the stupidity
Let's protect not destroy
Let's live together and enjoy
It doesn't have to be like this.

CHRISTINA ROSSETTI

The World

By day she woos me, soft, exceeding fair:

But all night as the moon so changeth she;

Loathsome and foul with hideous leprosy

And subtle serpents gliding in her hair.

By day she woos me to the outer air,

Ripe fruits, sweet flowers, and full satiety:

But through the night, a beast she grins at me,

A very monster void of love and prayer.

By day she stands a lie: by night she stands

In all the naked horror of the truth

With pushing horns and clawed and clutching hands.

Is this a friend indeed; that I should sell

My soul to her, give her my life and youth,

Till my feet, cloven too, take hold on hell?

JACQUI ROWE

Labels of the Otter

Finding him indistinguishable
from the current
they named him water.
*

Adrift, a raft of kits and dogs,
a family, bevy, lodge
a romp.
*

Death of otters
wears his name and Mr Spicer's
on a luggage tag.
*

The myth of lutra lutra
reconstructed from its kill
its waste its bones.
*

What Mr Spicer could not use
in 1844, without the skin or skill
to remake it.
*

Otr in his form of choice gorged on fish
till Loki did for him and filled his skin
with gold instead.
*

All around your head the rainclouds
like an umbrella, memento of your one
encounter with an otter.
*

Seven black otters and the dratsie king

grant you a wish to make them free.
Chuck His Majesty
under the chin,
snitch his skin
and disappear.
Never fear
the black black deeps.
*

St Cuthbert in the brine
waist deep endures because they come
to warm him with their breath
dry him with their fur.
*

Fish or flesh? What rabbit slips through streams?
Otter and chips is safe on Fridays
for your soul.
*

Full of play and gladness,
courage in duress,
four-footed, noblest soul
*

Evacuated from Warwickshire banks
with a label to bring him safe home
become, preserved a century,
a little model of a gas mask.

An otter's skull, from Spicer's taxidermy workshop in 19th century Warwick, was an exhibit in '60 Years of Collecting' at the Market Hall Museum, Warwick.

Ransom Note: Fox

the fox on the roof warm ticking
with blood isn't scared not an ahh

picture shiny haired extensive
litters the ones he selects to show
her from the paper nothing but
sincerity level with the lens

the sight he took her to
see a bonsai deer spritz
of energy and the man

held out to her
a fox it wasn't scared.

Black Swan Possibility

Drayton called the swans milk white,
redundant then, when all swans were,
though milk might rarely be so pure
as plumage silver in its flight
through streaky whey blue sky. Perhaps
the poet, loyal, sought to praise
the spotlessness of local cows
or did he ponder new found maps
their empty edge from where might creep
unthought of zoologica that grew
in all dimensions whole, as true
as monsters out of reason's sleep,
and in all spectra ever - never - seen
swans could be purple, red or green.

This poem appears on the Polesworth Poets Trail, in Pooley Country Park, Warwickshire. The poet Michael Drayton came from Polesworth.

Polesworth Swan

Nature but a shale that plays on ghostly strata
forms swan-shaped, this inscape of the self-healed
pool, ancient when the old ones gave up bronze, sky-
skimmer, water-sifter who fell down-
blossoming like breath of wintery god
legion in broken summer, seeding yearly
silver over early colonisers, layered
shallow as coal below unsoiled floor, speaking
and evading, sallow eyed,
that phantom touch of hand to beak
across striated distance, ages seamed
by tracks and ways, ice and reason,
sand spoil clay.

ALFRED LORD TENNYSON

The Eagle

He clasps the crag with crooked hands;
Close to the sun in lonely lands,
Ringed with the azure world, he stands.

The wrinkled sea beneath him crawls;
He watches from his mountain walls,
And like a thunderbolt he falls.

CLAIRE WALKER

They Keep A Cockatiel

When he was new he circled

the living room. They cheered his laps of honour

as he mastered the span of his wings.

He caught the shape of their tunes in his beak,

took their language as his own.

When I visited he'd greet me by their names.

He circled the living room too often. Learnt

no more songs - they had no more to teach- so left

him with only cuttle bones for small talk.

Their talk now is of how repetitive

shrieks frighten their children.

He still calls their names.

They say he is less pretty since

he started pulling out his feathers, ask me

why he does it.

The Behaviour of Other Animals

She likes her man like this, filled with the thirst

of the hunt. She runs her fingers down

the tracks of velvet lining his jacket, threads

the unassuming violet through

his buttonhole. She's heard it charms

the horses, keeps them calm under pressure. She wants

their muscular legs to keep pounding at any cost. Cares

not for the red-haired spirit of the woods.

She can almost feel him slipping the fur

round her shoulders, the fresh-caught

softness warming her neck.

When it happens she'll breathe the smell of it,

wonder why the scent of violets marks her skin.

JAN WATTS

CIRCUS

Safe in the roof bed
listen to the lions' roar.
Elephants trumpeting and trumping
in their big top.
The tent across the road and over the wall.
Bertram Mills has come to town again.

But let's make this general.
Not a particular circus in that part of town.
Not a travelling show
that tours around, just in summer months.

Our tunnel of love breathes fire,
but then the conjurer may announce
the arrival of those
who look up and depend on us
and deserving of healthy candy floss.

In theory,
you protect your children
from the lions.
If troubled times
overwhelm,
and you see teeth
you shield them.
Put the danger behind bars,
but they still see in.

See in? yes,
and they wear the T shirt
of their own show
that this talent

was too blind to see.
They see us prance and rear.
Performing for the ring master
with his top hat and whip.

Shielding them from our horseshit
is not a possibility.
They hear the acrobats' conversation.
They read that body language
of the human cannonball.
They observe all three rings
and worse,
they absorb.

Absorb like the keepers' sponge.
To acknowledge their knowledge
means that we need to confront.
We need to deal with it.

We are walking that tightrope.
A high wire we know well,
with fishnets ripped.
We are balanced.
But only just on one tippy toe.
Clubs to juggle.
Plates to twirl.
Hoops to whirl.
Sweating under the spot light
of no self-confidence.

The trapeze swings.
The feared fool flies so close, too close,
We will fall off.

So we pretend to our self
that they believe
our painted clown faces.

All is well we grin or
our circus will leave town.

It is not until our little audience has grown
that we realise that we did not protect them
from the spangles and the slapstick.

They saw all the performances,
Every one.
Now a new little audience.
I have fallen from my tightrope
and I am walking on wood shavings
In the ring again, but it is firm ground at last.
I will not ignore those who perform
with threatening jaws
for this next generation.
I will say 'no'.
I will speak up,
even if no one listens
to me banging the big drum.

WILLIAM WORDSWORTH

The Kitten and Falling Leaves

See the kitten on the wall, sporting with the leaves that fall,
Withered leaves—one—two—and three, from the lofty elder-tree!
Through the calm and frosty air, of this morning bright and fair . . .
—But the kitten, how she starts; Crouches, stretches, paws, and darts!

First at one, and then its fellow, just as light and just as yellow;
There are many now—now one—now they stop and there are none;
What intenseness of desire, in her upward eye of fire!

With a tiger-leap half way, now she meets the coming prey,
Lets it go as fast, and then, has it in her power again:
Now she works with three or four, like an Indian Conjuror;
Quick as he in feats of art, far beyond in joy of heart.

TOM WYRE

Inside Out

So you turn me inside out,
Turn my stomach without compassionate eyes.

Your brumal, brutal brazen blade,
An atrocity welded to your arm,
Tears at my skin, my dead mother's gift,
Her blessed cocoon tugged from my bones.

Shocked nerves convulse and shudder,
Flinching from your vice laden fingers,
Turned to talons, clawing with greed.
A sickening epitaph worn by vanity,
Their pockets bulge with empty cookies.

My muzzle mimics a cry for help.
So much pain, my dignity falls discarded,
As I scream, and I retch and I scream,
And my wretched blood streams,
And the tears of rain fill my gaze.

All this time as you stand on my head,
Your humanity lies buried on its head.
Your footprint lacks the soul
You once had when you were a child.
Your lost innocence, where did it go?
Once grazed mercy, twisted into scars.
Misplaced whispers upon a mandarin sunset.

Now I summon a stare into your eyes,
Searching for one reason, one answer,
My executioner, how much does the devil pay?
A candle's flicker burnt in an abysmal lantern,
A hope, its brightness devoured by the starved night,
By the darkness, the abyss behind your eyes.

As the light in my look fades to match yours,
I see your shredded smile lies bleeding on my fur.

Trophy Tooth

I remind you of your fear.
You watched me, tore me from my roots.
You ripped me from my home,
And the jaws of death.

A reluctant prize,
A memento for your warrior's pride,
Vanity eating away at you.

Your smile cut out bears the boar's tusk,
And as I look up at you from your clutching,
Grizzled, bitten now shaking hand,
I remind you of your fear.

Prism

I gaze at the azure roof and wonder as ethereal clouds wander by,
To spy smiles of starry silver that peek through the diaphanous sky.

Days of dreams embedded in reams fall from this poet's tongue,
Foolish reverie grabbed from slumber by autumnal gales,
Golden boughs wrenched from numbered brows of trees.
Faded grasses carpet the jaded earth,
To mirror the face of man, green with envy,
Locked in a spiral that never turns the key,
Ephemeral life's secret meant for eternity.
Mother Nature weeps reddened with blood of a thousand cuts for forests felled,
For her blighted animal and winged kin,

And for her bones poisoned in ignorance by a dabbling child.
Blue are the waves that sigh goodbye from a wailing sea.
Now you know why the sky cries,
And silence screams from nature's shaking heart.

Mankind needs to live up to its name and open eyes,
For in the darkness, blinding light is thumping on a door.

The Methuselah Tree

One is here, one is the tree,
Now I'm here, here I'm free,
Free to roam, free to float in time.
Spread my soul and see through my deep roots,
Fingers as dancing leaves weave tangled sins.
Wrapped green silk hides within my pithy within,
Cogent bark, wizened visage and wrinkled skin,
My twisted torso at one with cosmic kin.
Knotted parchment, notwithstanding my thoughts,
Exultant boughs bow to esoteric stars,
As the astral canopy mops my brow.
Rising sap, my soaring spirits leap to fly,
Raise my branches, my arms to the sun,
Yanking the yawning yet thundery sky.
Here, now and why?
Etching the sleepy sunset,
Gold god lays his head on flash in the pan clouds,
Dendritic lightning laid to rest.
Here, now and why?
A menagerie's palette of rustic dreams,
Echo as life paints and splashes screams,
As then and now a seed drops by my feet.
Swallowed by suckling soil it digests its birth,
And so one cycle encircles sole earth.

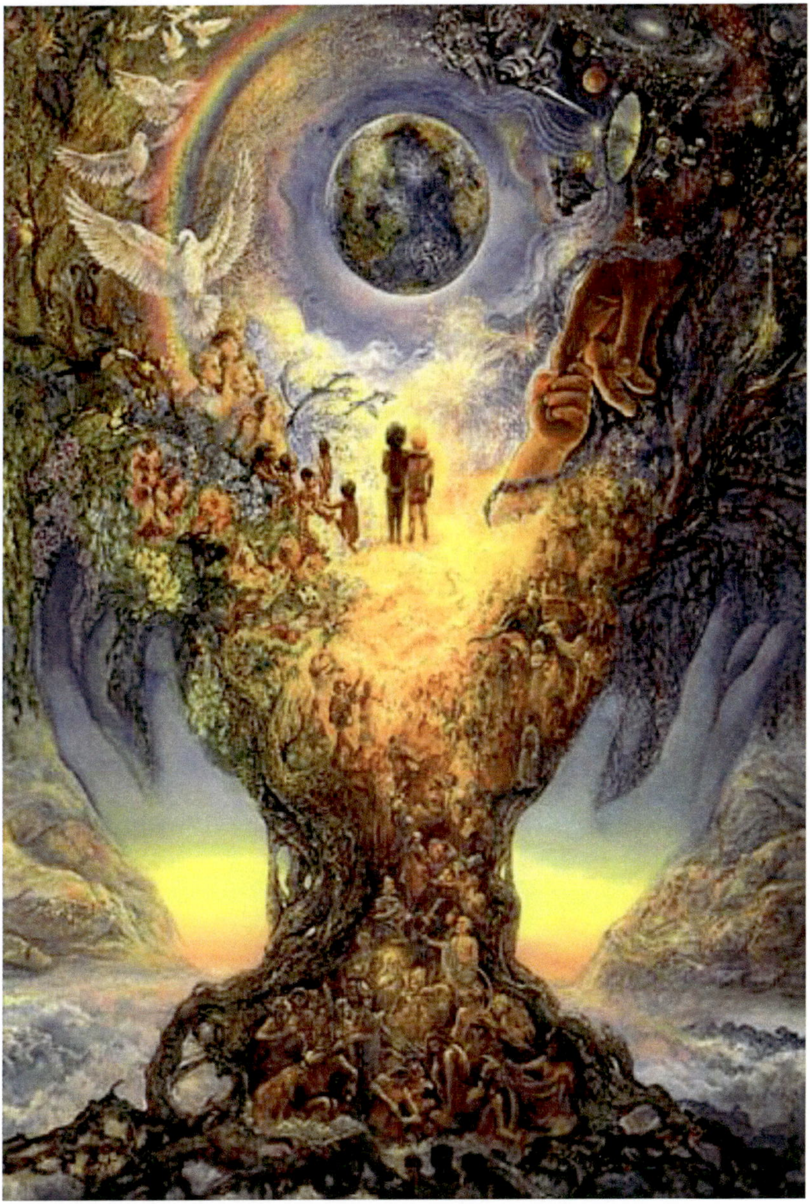

Surreal Green

Trees sway and bow to the winds in play,
Who would use their bark if they could sound dismay?
As swarms of leaves embark upon a random way,
And stinging nettles bite on their woe.

Grasses dance in moonlight's glance,
With captivated shadows held in defiance,
As the green man walks silently
On the mother's earthy skin,
Whilst she cuddles her time with a starlit grin,
To bury the sadness of environmental chagrin.

Innocence invisible to the silence,
Hidden from jealousy and greed,
Cast in a tumult of the flowers;
A posy that poses with the peacock,
And flutters in a riot of colours.

Glowing fish go green at the gills,
For the ocean's plug has been pulled,
Amorphous with insights and sounds fooled,
And with it the soulful guts have spilled.

Awakenings in the morning light.

Ella Wheeler Wilcox
From *Custer and Other Poems*, 1896

So many gods, so many creeds,
So many paths that wind and wind,
While just the art of being kind,
Is all the sad world needs.

BIOGRAPHIES

ILLUSTRATOR -JOSEPHINE WALL

Josephine Wall has kindly consented to letting us include her fantasy artwork for this book. More examples of her work and information about Josephine can be found on **www.josephinewall.co.uk**

Her paintings are mainly fantasies, influenced and inspired by the illustrative talents of Arthur Rackam, the surrealism of artists such as Magritte and Dali, and the romanticism of the pre-Raphaelites, which combined with her own imaginative ideas has led to a wide and varied range of work.

What are your views on nature and preservation?

Artists have been given a fabulous gift, but with it come great responsibilities. We have the chance to change the world by portraying images of how life could be and how it should be. No message is more powerful or has more impact than an image created by an artist driven by a desire to preserve all that is good in our world, and to vanquish all that is against nature. Yet another theme dear to my heart is to include a message encouraging conservation, as I wish that mankind would do everything possible to protect our precious and beautiful planet, and heal the damage we have already inflicted. My main concerns are pollution and de-forestation. I wish that man would no longer be ruled by greed, but just enjoy the simple things of life – most of which are free. We seem to be living in a throwaway world where skill and craftsmanship are undervalued. My Gaia paintings attempt to illustrate this feeling. "No More" and "Sadness of Gaia" portray the earth goddess protecting and repairing.

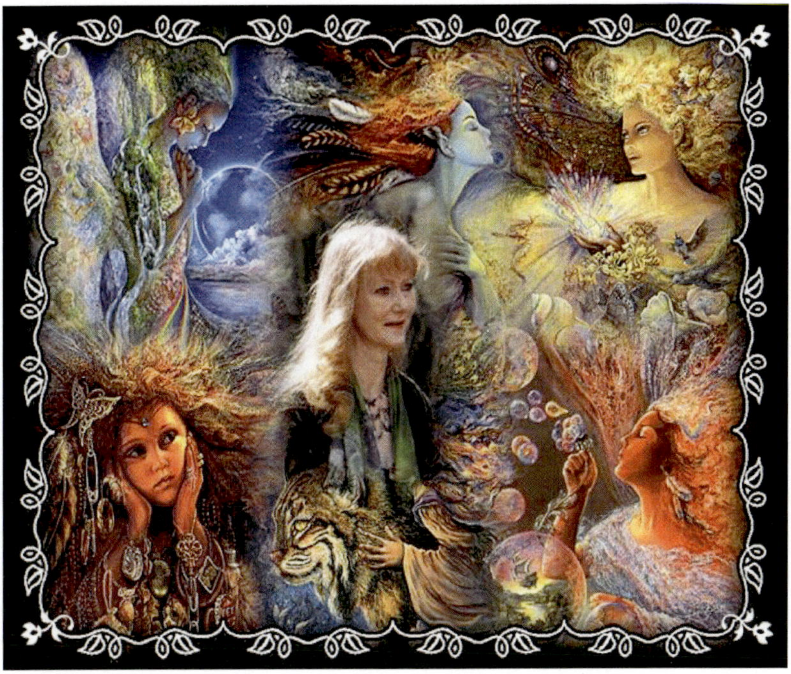

EDITOR - JACQUI ROWE

Jacqui Rowe is a professional poet. Her work has appeared extensively in leading magazines. Her published pamphlet collections are *Blue, Apollinaire* and *Paint.* In 2012 she won the Black Country Living Museum's international poetry competition. She is also co-editor, with Meredith Andrea, of Flarestack Poets, an independent press which in 2013 was named Publisher of the Year at the Michael Marks Poetry Pamphlet Awards and has twice published the Michael Marks Pamphlet of the Year, the first press to do so. Jacqui also works as a freelance editor, having edited, for example, Saleha Begum's *Ruptures and Fragments.* She is a workshop leader and a sought-after mentor, about whom former Birmingham Poet Laureate Charlie Jordan has said, "[Jacqui has] an ability to x-ray swiftly through a poem and see where it should be heading like a literary Satnav", as well as being a tutor for the Poetry School and poetry editor for the Writers' Workshop. Jacqui also produces and hosts Poetry Bites, a very popular Birmingham poetry night. She has considerable experience of working in the field of poetry and visual arts and heritage, having carried out a number of residencies, most recently having been appointed Writer in Residence in 2013 at the Barber Institute of Fine Arts in Birmingham. In 2014 she has been commissioned to run a series of workshops all over the UK in conjunction with leading theatre company TCTC's national tour of the First World War drama Regeneration. One of very few poets to have been trained by John Killick, internationally renowned authority on arts and dementia, a significant strand of her work is enabling older people in and out of care settings to see their words on paper. Having completed a Masters level module in Arts and Health at the University of Staffordshire, she also leads creative writing sessions with people with mental health issues, including NHS in-patients.
www.jacquirowe.com

'Drawing by Ruth Radcliffe'

FOREWORD - RICHARD BONFIELD

Richard Bonfield is Born Free's official Poet in Residence. Born and living in Leicester, Richard is a dazzling, accomplished poet with a deep love for the wild. A consummate writer, a virtuoso with words, his evocative, mesmerising poems feed the imagination, thrill the senses and frequently amuse.

"When Virginia McKenna asked me if I would like to be Poet in Residence my answer was a 'no brainer' as there was no doubt this was the ultimate accolade. It is to be asked to be Poet Laureate for the whole of suffering nature.

I feel that poetry could be the new Born Free... concentrating the hearts and minds of a new generation with a call to animal alms. Poetry really could change the planet...!

I see my new role as being that of a Pied Piper calling on a new generation of poets to dance the cosmic dance and lead all of us out of the sorry mess we now find ourselves in. The future is in our lyrical hands.

These are Richard's publications;

A Bestiary – an Animal Alphabet 1993

Swan for all Seasons….. 1997

Menagerie – 2004

Animated Nature – selected poems 1989-2009

Wildness – 2012

He has had some 300 different poems published in over 30 magazines countrywide.

THE INSPIRATION - ELAINE CATHERINE CHRISTIE

Elaine Catherine Christie is a published poet, ACTIVATOR, Member and Fundraiser with Born Free Foundation. She plays an active role with many charities on animal issues and has a City & Guilds in Animal Care. Her first poem was highly recommended in Mid-Warwickshire Mind and S.W.U.F. Poetry Competition, her second poem came 5th in Voices.net International Poetry Competition, in 2005. She won first prize and third prize in alternate issues of *Trust Talk*. Elaine's poetry has appeared in college pamphlets, *Arts All Over the Place, First Time, Dial 174, WWF Earth book, United Press, Forward Poetry, Animal Antics, Poetry Rivals 2011*, online and currently on Born Free Foundation's website. Elaine has organised and hosted poetry events to raise funds for rescued animals for Born Free Foundation.

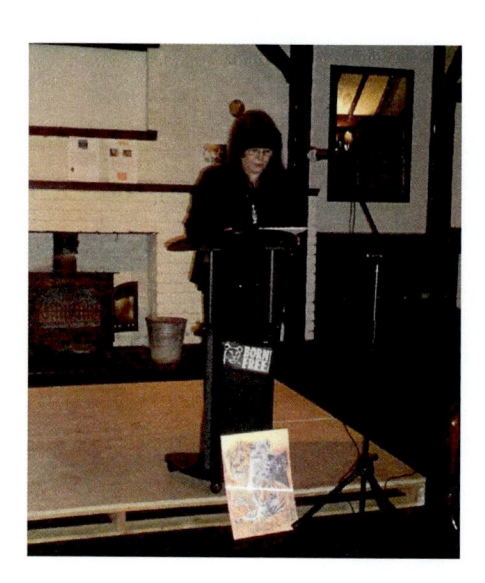

CONTRIBUTORS

Janine Allen is a Certified Professional Dog Trainer and Rescue Me Dog's professional dog trainer. Janine's passion is working with people and their dogs. She provides demonstrations for those who have adopted shelter dogs, lends email support to adopted dog owners who need information beyond Training Support Pages, and aids shelter staff and volunteers in understanding dog behaviour to increase their adoptability. www.RescueMeDog.org

Mike Alma Having written, very privately, for the last 50 years, writing a family history reignited his enthusiasm, leading him to join writers' circles and, for the first time, sharing his words with other, like-minded, people. *Short Stories from Black Pear*, published by Black Pear Publishing, Worcester 2014 (3 short stories); *Flashes of Fiction*, the Worcestershire Literary Festival 2013 Flash Fiction anthology; *You Can't Be Serious*, an anthology of humour 2013, from the Worcester Writers' Circle (2 short stories); *Coachlines* Issue 13 anthology 2014 (poetry and prose) from Coachhouse Writers, Stourbridge.

Jude Ashworth has been writing for several years now and finds it exhilarating. She is the Facilitator of a creative writing group called Pens of Erdington which meets 1st and 3rd Wednesday of each month at Erdington Library's Community Room 1-3 pm and is free. The group has just published a creative writing Anthology (£4.50) including some of her work. She loves to read her work at performance poetry venues such as Poetry Bites and Poetry at Lunch at the Library of Birmingham.

David Barber is from Birmingham and comes from a family of artists, he is wild about Wilde. He has had poems published in 19 different anthologies by United Press. He is a painter and poet and working on his first collection.

William Blake (28 November 1757 – 12 August 1827) was an English painter, poet and printmaker. Born in Soho, London, he was the third of seven children, two of whom died in infancy. Because of his headstrong temperament that he was not sent to school but instead enrolled in drawing classes. He also made excursions into poetry and at the age of 21, he became a professional engraver. Blake married Catherine Boucher who proved an invaluable aid throughout his life, helping to print his illuminated works and maintaining his spirits throughout numerous misfortunes. Blake's first collection of poems, *Poetical Sketches,* was printed around 1783. In 1788, Blake experimented with relief etching, a method he used to produce most of his books, paintings, pamphlets and poems. In 1804 he began to write and illustrate *Jerusalem* (1804–20), his most ambitious work. Blake is held in high regard by later critics for his expressiveness and creativity, and for the philosophical and mystical undercurrents within his work. In 2002, Blake was placed at number 38 in the BBC's poll of 100 Greatest Britons.

Elizabeth Barrett Browning (6 March 1806 – 29 June 1861) was one of the most prominent English poets of the Victoria era. Her poetry was widely popular in both Britain and the United States during her lifetime. At 15 Elizabeth Barrett became ill, suffering from intense head and spinal pain for the rest of her life, rendering her frail. She took laudanum for the pain, which may have led to a lifelong addiction. She met and corresponded with the writer Robert Browning, who admired her work. The courtship and marriage between the two were carried out in secret, for fear of her father's disapproval. Following the wedding she was disinherited by her father and rejected by her brothers. The couple moved to Italy in 1846, where she would live for the rest of her life. They had one son, Robert Barrett Browning, whom they called Pen. Towards the end of her life, her lung function worsened, and she died in Florence in 1861. A collection of her last poems was published by her husband shortly after her death.

George Gordon, Lord Byron (22 January 1788 – 19 April 1824) was born into a rapidly fading aristocratic family. A clubfoot from birth left him self-conscious most of his life. After receiving a scathing review of his first volume of poetry, *Hours of Idleness*, in 1808, Byron retaliated with the satirical poem "English Bards and Scotch Reviewers." The poem attacked the literary community with wit and satire, and gained him his first literary recognition. Among Byron's best-known works are the lengthy narrative poems *Don Juan* and *Childe Harold's Pilgrimage,* and the short lyric *She Walks in Beauty.* He travelled all over Europe especially in Italy where he lived for seven years and then joined the Greek War of Independence. He died at age 36 from a fever contracted while in Missolonghi in Greece.

David Calcutt is a novelist, playwright and poet. He has written adaptations for theatre and BBC Radio 4. His play *Gifts of Flame* won the Sacred Earth Drama Award. He has plays published by Nelson Thorns and Oxford University Press; OUP has also published 2 of his novels. Road Kill is a poetry collaboration with Nadia Kingsley on woodland animals and folklore. His one man play 'Tales from the Tat Man' is replaying in October around Birmingham. David's poetry appears widely in print.

Helen Calcutt is a poet, dance artist and journalist. She is the author of '*Sudden rainfall'* her first collection of poetry, published by experimental English publishing house Perdika Press. Calcutt's creative and critical work has been published globally, featuring in journals such as *Equinox, The London Magazine, Poetry Scotland, Fused, Bare Fiction,* and the *Wales Arts Review.* Her new project ecriture corporelle – a 'bodily writing' launches at the internationally acclaimed Poetry International Festival this year, and explores dance & poetry as a unified art form.

Gilbert Keith Chesterton (29 May 1874 – 14 June 1936) better known as **G.K. Chesterton**, was born in London, England on the 29th of May, 1874. Though he considered himself a mere "rollicking journalist," he was actually a prolific and gifted writer in virtually every area of literature. A man of strong opinions and enormously talented at defending them, his exuberant personality nevertheless allowed him to maintain warm friendships with people - such as George Bernard Shaw and H. G. Wells - with whom he vehemently disagreed. In 1931, the BBC, invited Chesterton to give a series of radio talks. He accepted, tentatively at first. However, from 1932 until his death, Chesterton delivered over 40 talks per year. He was allowed (and encouraged) to improvise on the scripts. This allowed his talks to maintain an intimate character, as did the decision to allow his wife and secretary to sit with him during his broadcasts. Chesterton wrote around 80 books, several hundred poems, some 200 short stories, 4000 essays, and several plays. He was a columnist for the *Daily News*, the *Illustrated London News*, and his own paper, *G. K.'s Weekly*; he also wrote articles for the *Encyclopædia Britannica*, including the entry on Charles Dickens and part of the entry on Humour in the 14th edition (1929). While *The Man Who Was Thursday* is arguably his best-known novel. Near the end of his life, Pope Pius XI invested Chesterton as Knight Commander with Star of the Papal Order of St. Gregory the Great.

Chyi Yu is a retired Chinese singer and, as her song *Donde Voy* was dedicated to the dogs murdered in China, we have used this under the Fair Use Law. It also appears on the Animal Liberation Front's website.

Emily Dickinson was born on December 10, 1830, in Amherst, Massachusetts. While Dickinson was a prolific private poet, fewer than a dozen of her nearly eighteen hundred poems were published during her lifetime and the work that was published was usually altered significantly by the publishers to fit the conventional poetic rules of the time. Throughout her life, she seldom left her home and visitors were few. While Dickinson was extremely prolific as a poet and regularly enclosed poems in letters to friends, she was not publicly recognized during her lifetime. She died in Amherst in 1886.Upon her death, Dickinson's family discovered forty hand bound volumes of nearly 1,800 poems. The first volume of her work was published posthumously in 1890 and the last in 1955.

Des (A LONE WOLF) please pass this on to enlighten those oblivious to the plight of the great and wonderful wolves of Alaska! Animal Liberation Front.

Eugene Egan Lives in Moseley, Birmingham and studied Journalism at Solent University in Southampton. He is a political activist, writer, mental health activist, raising awareness to reduce the stigma surrounding mental health. He enjoys reading and writing poetry, using it as therapy in dealing with depression. He also cares about the natural world. Moved by animal abuse, he hopes his poetry will be food for thought and help bring about a change in attitude towards animals.

Giovanni 'Spoz' Esposito is from Rubery, Birmingham. His *Poetry in Motions* CD appeared in 2004 and *The Day the Earth Grew Hair*, his poetry collection, which is hugely comical with a child-like view, came out in 2008. He was Birmingham's Poet Laureate for 2006/2007. He is an award winning performance poet, singer/songwriter, film maker, and playwright. He has appeared on television, radio and performed at the Glastonbury Festival, Cheltenham Literature Festival, Oxford Literature Festival, Warwick Words Festival, Ledbury Poetry Festival. He continues to work in schools up and down the country, lifting the appeal of writing and performance poetry. **www.spoz.net**

Chris Fewings lives in Birmingham and writes poems, stories (including *a Glossary of my Grandmother*) and articles. He also hosts poetry groups at Balsall Heath Library and elsewhere. His pamphlet of poems loosely based around the Rea Valley in Birmingham has been long- listed for the Cafe Writers Commission. **www.chris.fewin.gs**

Caroline Gill's poetry chapbook, *The Holy Place*, co-authored with John Dotson, was commissioned and published by Peter Thabit Jones, editor of *The Seventh Quarry* (Swansea) and Stanley H. Barkan, editor of *Cross-Cultural Communications* (New York) in 2012. Caroline won the international Petra Kenney Poetry Competition (General Section) in 2007. She gained Third Place in the 2009 Haddon Library Competition, launched to mark the 800th anniversary of the University of Cambridge. Caroline is an External Collaborator for the Romanian magazine, *Orizont Literar Contemporan*. The natural world, in all its wonder and fragility, remains a constant source of inspiration. **www.carolinegillpoetry.com**

Oliver Wendell Holmes (August 29, 1809 – October 7, 1894) Born in Cambridge, Massachusetts, Holmes was an American physician, poet, professor, lecturer, and author based in Boston. He began writing poetry at an early age. For his literary achievements and other accomplishments, he was awarded numerous honorary degrees from universities around the world. Holmes's writing often commemorated his native Boston area, and much of it was meant to be humorous or conversational. He was often called upon to issue occasional poetry, or poems written specifically for an event. In 1891 Holmes died quietly after falling asleep in the afternoon of Sunday, October 7, 1894. As his son wrote, "His death was as peaceful as one could wish for those one loves."

Rangzeb Hussain lives in Birmingham, and works in a secondary school. He has been influenced by his grandmother, who would tell stories under the moonlit skies of a village in Pakistan, and he would dream of flying carpets and high adventure. Rangzeb's grandmother also inspired his love for animals and nature. She believed in respecting the natural world, and always taught him that humans are gardeners and protectors of the animal kingdom. Her words of wisdom continue to inspire him to this day, her songs and voice live on through his poetry.

Sarah James is an award-winning poet, short fiction writer and journalist. Her first collection *Into the Yell* (Circaidy Gregory Press, 2010) won third prize in the International Rubery Book Awards 2011. A second, more experimental collection, *Be[yond]*, is published by Knives, Forks and Spoons Press. She believes the pressing need to protect the world and wildlife around us should not be ignored. Her website is at: **www.sarah-james.co.uk**

Janet Jenkins is a retired Nursery Head Teacher, from Hednesford, Staffordshire. She is a one of the founder members of the Lichfield Poets and has taken part in all group performances including The Lichfield Festivals, The Lichfield Mysteries and Wolverhampton City Voices. She has poems in the group's anthologies – *Silver Words* and *Battle Lines* – and in *The Mortal Man* (Anthology for The National Autistic Society) Her work has also been included in *Be Magazine* and *Hearing Voices*.

Nina Lewis is a published poet who works as a teacher and Assistant Writer for Writing West Midlands. Nina performs her poetry at various venues across the Midlands and beyond. She has recently had a poem accepted on the Wenlock Poetry Trail and a series of haiku are being used as part of an exhibition for 'What's the Agenda?' at the MAC. Nina's writing covers a range of subjects including social commentary on issues close to her heart.

Tessa Kate Lowe grew up in South Africa (with the shongalulus). She has lived in Birmingham for forty six years and now loves it. She has had two pamphlets published and she is an avid open-miker!

Charlotte Mew (15 November 1869 – 24 March 1928) Mew's work spans the cusp between Victorian poetry and Modernism. She was born in Bloomsbury, London. Her father died in 1898 without making adequate provision for his family; two of her siblings suffered from mental illness, and three others died in early childhood leaving Charlotte, her mother and her sister, Anne. Charlotte and Anne made a pact never to marry for fear of passing on insanity to their children. Through most of her adult life, Mew wore masculine attire and kept her hair short, adopting the appearance of a dandy. Mew gained the patronage of several literary figures, notably Thomas Hardy, who called her the best woman poet of her day. After the death of her sister from cancer in 1927, she descended into a deep depression and eventually committed suicide.

Matt Nunn is a poet and a creative writing and poetry tutor working in adult education, mental health and beyond. He has been a published poet for over 20 years and has performed at poetry events all over the country. He has read his work on BBC Radio 3 amongst others and performed his poetry on both BBC and ITV. He is a Warwick university fellow in creative writing and was the poet-in-residence at Birmingham City FC. He is the author of 3 poetry collections, *Apocalyptic Bubblegum* (MAP 2003), *Happy 'cos I'm Blue* (Heaventree 2006) and *Sounds in the Grass* (Nine Arches Press 2009). He lives in some kind of bliss with his wife and two children in Solihull.

Antony Owen is from Coventry, England. His first collection was *My Father's Eyes were Blue*. His 2nd collection *The Dreaded Boy* was published by Pighog Press in 2011. Owen was a 2011 poetry competition finalist in The Wilfred Owen Story. His latest collection is a collaboration with Joseph Horgan *The Year I Loved England,* also by Pighog Press.

Malini Patel This poem was kindly given to us by the Animal Liberation Front.

Jade Phipps is a thirty year old black British female, born and in Birmingham and from a Caribbean descent. After growing up attending Birmingham's Stage 2 youth theatre and the National Youth Theatre she went to live in London at the age of 18. Jade went to Mountview Academy of Dramatic Arts where she acquired a 2.1 degree in drama. After living in London for 11 years she is now back in her hometown with a new-found love of poetry and playing the ukulele.

Clare Powers This poem was written by Clare in 1999 when she was just 14 when she was at school for a collection of poetry by various schools in the West Midlands.

Christina Rossetti (5 December 1830 – 29 December 1894) was an English poet who wrote a variety of romantic, devotional, and children's poems. She is perhaps best known for her long poem *Goblin Market,* her love poem *Remember,* and for the words of the Christmas Carol *In the Bleak Midwinter* Rossetti was one of four children of Italian parents. When she was 14, Rossetti suffered a nervous breakdown and left school. Bouts of depression and related illness followed. Rossetti sat for several of Dante Rossetti's most famous paintings. In 1848, she was the model for the Virgin Mary in his first completed oil painting. She was opposed to slavery (in the American South), cruelty to animals (in the prevalent practice of animal experimentation), and the exploitation of girls in underage prostitution. She died in Bloomsbury on 29 December 1894 and was buried in Highgate Cemetery.

Alfred, Lord Tennyson (6 August 1809 – 6 October 1892) was Poet Laureate during much of Queen Victoria's reign and remains one of the most popular British poets. Tennyson excelled at penning short lyrics, such as "Break, Break, Break", "The Charge of the Light Brigade", "Tears Idle Tears" and "Crossing the Bar". Much of his verse was based on classical mythological themes, such as "Ulysses", although *In Memoriam A.H.H.* was written to commemorate his best friend Arthur Hallam, a fellow poet and fellow student at Trinity College, Cambridge, who was engaged to Tennyson's sister, but died from a brain haemorrhage before they could marry. Tennyson also wrote some notable blank verse, including *Idylls of the King*, "*Ulysses*", and "*Tithonus*". After William

Wordsworth's death in 1850, Tennyson was appointed to the position of Poet Laureate, he held the position until his own death in 1892, by far the longest tenure of any laureate before or since. He died on 6 October 1892 at Aldworth, aged 83. He was buried in Westminster Abbey.

William Wordsworth (7 April 1770 – 23 April 1850) was a major English Romantic poet who, with Samuel Taylor Coleridge, helped to launch the Romantic Movement in English literature with the 1798 joint publication *Lyrical Ballads*. Wordsworth's love of nature is reflected in his poems, particularly those written in the Lake District, where he lived for a time with his sister Dorothy in Dove Cottage in Grasmere. His most ambitious work was *The Prelude*, a long autobiographical poem. In 1791, Wordsworth visited France, where he became enthralled with the Republican movement. In 1843, he reluctantly accepted the post of Poet Laureate, which he remained until his death from pleurisy in 1850.

Claire Walker's poetry has appeared in various print and online publications including *The Interpreter's House, Ink Sweat and Tears, Hearing Voices* and *Emerge Literary Journal*. In June 2013 she won third place in the 2013/2014 Worcestershire Poet Laureate Competition.

Jan Watts was the 16th Poet Laureate in 2011-2012. Jan has a background in teaching Creative Writing, Drama and Performing Arts in schools, adult education and prisons. She was Writer in Residence at HMYOI Swinfen Hall. She has an MPhil in Playwriting from the University of Birmingham. Her plays have been performed in England, Scotland and New Zealand and she has a poetry collection called *Empty Talk!* Published. As well as being tutor/mentor of Erdington Library's Creative Writing Group, she organised the successful Erdington Library's Writers' Retreat and is currently working on future ones. She currently runs Poetry for Lunch at Birmingham's new Library and has just released her novel *Benches*.

Tom Wyre is Staffordshire Poet Laureate 2013 -14 and is also a prize recipient of Walsall Mayor's Poetry Awards. Wyre performed at the prestigious O'Bheal poetry event, Cork, Ireland in July 2013. A new book complete with CD *Through the Lucid Door* was published in 2013.

BORN FREE
30
YEARS FOR WILDLIFE

The President of Born Free USA Adam Roberts

has given us this statement -

'Our affiliated organisation in America, Born Free USA, has a major campaign on all aspects of the fur trade. This includes stopping the use of the most egregious and brutal forms of furbearer trapping in the wild, such as the steel jaw leghold trap; ending fur farming in America and throughout Europe (they are a major player in the Fur Free Alliance); stopping trapping on National Wildlife Refuges in America; and, of course, stopping the international trade in wild animal furs including tigers, Canadian lynx, and other species.'

Born Free Foundation
3 Grove House, Foundry Lane
, Horsham, RH13 5PL, UK - Charity Reg. No. 1070906